THE NANNY TEXTBOOK

THE NANNY TEXTBOOK

THE PROFESSIONAL NANNY GUIDE TO CHILD CARE 2003

A.M. Merchant

Writer's Showcase
New York Lincoln Shanghai

The Nanny Textbook
The Professional Nanny Guide To Child Care 2003

Writer's Showcase
an imprint of iUniverse, Inc.

For information address:
iUniverse
2021 Pine Lake Road, Suite 100
Lincoln, NE 68512
www.iuniverse.com

ISBN: 0-595-26138-8 (Pbk)
ISBN: 0-595-65532-7 (Cloth)

Printed in the United States of America

Contents

Introduction vii

Acknowledgements ix

PART ONE   *Professional Skills*

   CHAPTER ONE   *Keys to Making the Relationship Work* 3

   CHAPTER TWO   *Roles & Responsibilities* 20

   CHAPTER THREE   *Professional Nanny Process* 27

   CHAPTER FOUR   *Communication* 54

   CHAPTER FIVE   *Ethics for Child Care Professionals* 74

PART TWO   *Child Development Skills*

   CHAPTER SIX   *Keeping Children Safe* 83

   CHAPTER SEVEN   *Growth & Development*
                            Erikson and Developmental Psychology 106

   CHAPTER EIGHT   *High Self-Esteem and*
                            the Developing Child 118

   CHAPTER NINE   *Curriculum & Creative Play* 128

   CHAPTER TEN   *Mothers & Babies Common Concerns I* 146

   CHAPTER ELEVEN   *Toddlers & Older Children*
                            Common Concerns II 159

PART THREE   *Home Health Care Skills*

   CHAPTER TWELVE   *Nutrition* *179*

   CHAPTER THIRTEEN   *Hygiene* *195*

   CHAPTER FOURTEEN   *Common Pediatric Illnesses* *208*

   CHAPTER FIFTEEN   *Managing Stress* *229*

   CHAPTER SIXTEEN   *Principles of Home Hygiene &
                        Management* *242*

   About the Author *251*

   Index..*253*

Tables, Charts & Forms   **Page**

Professional Nanny Process Form   31
Nanny's Sample Weekly Schedule   51
Nanny's Daily Log Form   69
Fire Escape Plan   101
Safety Statistics   103
Safety Resources   104
Midlife Adjustment Chart   115
Learning Styles Table   121
Growth & Development Forms   142–145
Potty Training Outline   161
Vitamin Mineral Chart   184
Monitoring Child's Hearing   218
EZ Dose It Medication Chart   225
Emergency Information Form   226
Consent Authorization Form   227
First Aid Supply Checklist   228
Social Readjustment Rating Table   229
Stressors & Effects Table   234

Introduction

The original edition of this Manual; *The Professional Nanny Guide to Childcare* was published in 1987 and quickly became a staple in nanny training programs. From Australia to New England and through-out the Midwest, the vast majority of nanny training programs listed the *Professional Nanny Guide to Childcare* as required reading.

Several editions have been published since then, but have only been available to a small group of organizations in New England. With this edition, The Manual is available for worldwide distribution and prom-ises to once again become required reading for nanny training pro-grams everywhere. The curriculum is based upon more than two decades of research and covers all of the essential fundamental princi-ples of in-home childcare. It is a basic reference for anyone employed to care for children and for parents wishing to learn what to expect from a professional nanny. For those pursuing the establishment of standards for in-home childcare, *The Professional Nanny Guide to Childcare* pro-vides a basis for formalizing standards of care in the home.

The Professional Nanny Guide to Childcare is the required textbook for Professional Nanny Online (PNO), the tuition-free distance training pro-gram for nannies worldwide. *The Professional Nanny Guide to Childcare* is based on the curriculum first recognized by the Massachusetts Department of Public Health, Division of Health Care Quality in 1981 for Homemakers/Home Health Aides.

Acknowledgements

This Nanny Textbook was developed and has evolved over the years because of the support, advice, guidance and dedication of some very important people. My children, Rick & Ken, have effectively served as research subjects growing up, until they, along with Jeff & Kelsey became old enough to help proof read & edit the various editions of *The Nanny Textbook*. From the time they were babies and as the children were growing up, our home essentially functioned as a nanny training school. It was not unusual for us to have as many as five nannies and one housekeeper living with us, at any given time.

Nor is it an understatement to say that watching the children grow up under the care & supervision of numerous nannies provided the kind of experience which could only be found in our home. The third floor of the eight bedroom Victorian where hundreds of nannies resided upon their arrival in Boston was affectionately referred to as Nannyland.

Sheri Goddard and Melissa Blom Baxter, our two executive nannies for many years, deserve special acknowledgement. As Rick & Kenny's personal nannies, they sized up all new arrivals to the Professional Nanny Training Program before they were allowed to interact with any of the children.

Professional Nanny, Sally Tingley Walker has been involved with the Professional Nanny Training Program since the early 1990's and more recently Professional Nanny Online. Sally's dedication to the nanny profession & her love of learning has been a strong motivating factor in the development of this book.

Debbie Davis, founding member & the first president of the International Nanny Association actively encouraged the first edition of this book and has made numerous suggestions about content since then.

Wendy Sachs of The Philadelphia Nanny Network and former four term president of the International Nanny Association has reviewed past editions of the *Nanny Textbook* and made many excellent suggestions that are still reflected in the pages of this edition.

Dr. Benjamin Spock is especially acknowledged here for his sage advice, his wit and his wisdom over the years. Many other contributors to the *Nanny Text* should be acknowledged; Dr. Mike Meyerhoff and Dr. Lucian Richard who also taught classes for our nannies over the years.

The help, support and inspiration of all of these people has helped shape and refine not only the *Nanny Textbook 2003*, but also, Professional Nanny Online (PNO), the distance training program it was written to support.

The most significant person, however in the development of the *Nanny Textbook*, the development of PNO, and in the relentless pursuit of the highest standards when it comes to caring for our children, is my consultant and best friend, William Geissler. He deserves credit and acknowledgement for his tireless work and his steadfast belief that those who care for our children deserve the utmost respect and recognition.

PART ONE

Professional Skills

CHAPTER ONE

Keys to Making the Relationship Work

Introduction

The relationship between the nanny and the parent is unlike almost any other employer/employee relationship. In any other line of work most people would react to the suggestion of actually living with their boss, with either belly-laughter, or horror. Yet it is common in this field, and it can work very successfully. For those who live elsewhere, but work all day in their employer's private home, the job is less dynamic than it would be had they decided to "live-in", but it is still more dynamic than for those who actually work in a school, or center.

The relationships which work, have some common denominators. First and foremost, there is mutual RESPECT for one another. Neither the parent, nor the nanny considers ones self to be the more valuable human being. In other words, there is consideration for the others wants, needs and time. The relationships which work are the ones where the parties are more involved in what they can give, rather than what they can take (or get away with, or take advantage of, etc.). If you know of a family who has had a lot of success with their child care arrangement, 99% of those people are "givers". The same is true for the nanny who seems to always end up in the best situations, almost 100% of the time, she's a "giver".

The parent or the nanny who is super-critical, or even just very picky will undoubtedly always find something to be dissatisfied about. There are those who are defensive, perhaps justifiably so, because they had a prior poor experience. When these people are in transition, they may inadvertently create enough discomfort among those they interview, because of the nature of their questions, to get rejected.

Those with successful past parent/nanny relationships haven't been successful because they didn't have their problems. It worked because the people involved are solution-seekers. Perhaps because they are respectful of one another, instead of fault-finding, blaming and catastrophizing. They look immediately to solutions when problems come up. Most of the time, they find the solutions they're looking for and the result is that the relationship works and has longevity.

At Professionalnanny.com we have many times heard a parent or a nanny say "So and so has had such good Luck". Be advised, it has nothing whatsoever to do with luck. That's like saying that someone's marriage worked because they were "lucky".

To follow are some guidelines for some very common issues which occur between nannies and parents. Research Project Workbooks (RPW's) per chapter as well as all references to forms for orientating a nanny to a new position can be obtained at www.professionalnanny.com

Work Agreement

This is a necessity and it is the parent's responsibility to prepare the work agreement and present it to the nanny. Typical clauses included in a standard nanny-family agreement are hours, salary, benefits, duration, etc. Go to www.professionalnanny.com for a sample contract, or call Professionalnanny.com at 508-650-8889. The work agreement should be completed by the parent(s) for the nanny, before the nanny begins caring for their children.

Daily Log Binder

Every home should have a special binder containing daily notes on each child. In addition to keeping a daily log, emergency medical information on each child should be in the binder, along with emergency telephone numbers, as well as recipes, menus, playgroup/activities schedules, and car pool information. The binder should be kept in the kitchen where all adults have access to it. Refer to the chapter on Communication for a sample Daily Log and Common Pediatric Illnesses for emergency forms.

Transition To A New Position

Once a position has been accepted, getting to know each other is the next big step. If the family has more than one child, its a good idea to structure the transition so that time can be spent with one child at a time. Children are naturally competitive when it comes to the significant adults in their lives and its easier to focus on one child at a time. Perhaps a morning with one, and then the afternoon with the other can be arranged. This will make a big difference starting on the first full day of work. Each child will have had an opportunity to get to know you and vice versa. You'll feel more comfortable with them, thus more confident, and it will show.

Orientation To The Family

However formal this may sound it is important for the Nanny who is working in a private home to be thoroughly oriented. Parents should assist you with the process of orientation using the forms included in the Professional Nanny Online Workbook; "Orientation To The Family". These forms aren't intended to be a knowledge assessment, but rather an efficient way to get to know the children and the environment. Parents should also complete the Orientation to Family "Process" forms to be certain that you have the information you need to get off on the right foot. Keep in mind that routine is very important to children, especially young children. The more you know about the family members and the home, the less stress everyone will feel. There are a few very important topics to address first when starting a job in your employer's home.

1. *Safety Assessment*—Refer to the <u>Home Safety Assessment</u> form, found in the Keeping Children Safe chapter whenever a new job begins. Nannies should conduct a Home Safety Assessment every six weeks, or more often—but always when a new job begins in order to familiarize yourself with the new setting.

2. *Emergency Overview*—Refer to the <u>Emergencies and First Aid</u> form (found in the Workbook: "Orientation To The Family"), or after reviewing the book, "A Sigh Of Relief", or a similar book on pediatric first aid, answer the questions on the form. This won't take the place of a first aid course, but it will be a great review for those who have taken first aid. For those who haven't taken a first aid course, you should take one at your earliest opportunity. Anyone caring for children for compensation should not only have first aid, but CPR certification as well. In the meantime, this exercise will raise your consciousness and make you more aware of potential hazards. An emergency medical information form should be completed by a parent and kept in the "Daily Log" binder, as should emergency telephone numbers.

3. *Growth & Development Orientation Assignments*—The <u>Description of the Child's Current Development</u> form (found in the Professional Nanny Online Workbook; "Orientation To The Family") is used to determine where the child is developmentally. Using the information you have completed on this form (parent can assist you with this), go on to the "Safety Considerations Relative to the Child's Development". You now should know what is and what is not a safety hazard. The next form "Creative Play", will help you become oriented to the child's favorite activities and is a good place to document what you would like to suggest. The "Anticipated Development Changes" form will help you assess future changes. Reviewing/researching such information

will help you plan new activities and will sensitize you to look for and encourage the child's changing developmental needs. Some of the Information requested will require you to ask specific questions, review portions of The Nanny Text and also, perhaps to do research. The purpose is to help the transition into caring for children.

4. *Process Recording*—The process is an organized communication exercise which is used to initiate a discussion regarding: privacy, should you accept a position in a private home (either on a live-in, or on a live-out basis), etc. It can also be used to open the discussion of other issues. Its purpose is to help set a healthy, open line of communication right from the start of your employment. See the chapter on Communication for an in-depth discussion.

Working With The New Mother

Few new moms anticipate the ambivalence they will feel when the time comes for them to return to work and leave the baby with the Nanny. It is common to see anxiety on the part of the new mother, which manifests in what appears to be a lack of confidence in the Nanny, distrust or general irritability. Needless to say, this doesn't do a lot for the relationship, especially at this early stage. Empathy is what's needed in these situations as well as some planning to help avoid this problem. It helps if the Nanny is hired in enough time prior to the start of the job to enable her to spend some time with the mother and baby. We suggest that the Nanny spend several days with the mom, getting to know her and the baby's routine. As everyone becomes more comfortable, encourage mom to let you care for the baby while she does errands, etc. Gradually increasing the amount of time that you are caring for the baby is the ideal scenario and works extremely well. Be sure you are as attentive to the things on which the mother puts emphasis. This will help her feel more comfortable and trusting. There may be things she wants you to do, or precautions to take, which you may not think are important. Do it anyway. Taking some extra time with something, or going out of your way is a small price to pay to help the new mom feel more comfortable as she makes the adjustment from home to work.

Privacy

These should always be discussed before starting the job. The Professional Nanny Online Workbook, entitled; "Orientation to Family" contains a communication exercise called a Process Recording, which is helpful once the job has been accepted. Every job is different and you may need to think through the privacy element before you can decide if a particular job is right for you. Think about other situations you have worked in, lived in, or otherwise experienced. What were your "pet peeves" in those situations? What are your morning, evening, weekend habits that you enjoy and may not be willing to change? What about mealtime? How will it change with this job? What If the family prefers to eat alone, or just the parents prefer to eat alone? Your habits should be compared with theirs and discussed. Let the family know that you want to honor their particular family rituals. Give them permission to tell you what it is they really prefer. This will make it easier for you to tell them more about what your needs are.

Curfews

When the Nanny lives in a family's home, the topic of curfew may come up. A responsible adult will not require another adult to set limits. There are, however some instances where it makes sense for all members residing in a home to be in at a particular time. For instance, dogs may bark and wake up family members or neighbors when someone comes in late. Some homes have alarm systems to reset. Parents know that when they have had too little sleep they may be impatient, slow to respond, not interact with the child and perhaps create a safety hazard. If you are out until one or two o'clock in the morning, they may feel worried and anxious while they are at work and wonder if you fell asleep while dinner was cooking. It makes sense to avoid situations that may alter judgment. A responsible nanny sould always be in at a reasonable hour which is an indication that the nanny possesses good judgment and takes her work responsibilities seriously

Automobile As A Benefit

In many situations, the family/employer provides a car for the Nanny to use when transporting the children and/or for the Nanny's personal use. Cars are expensive to purchase, to maintain and to insure. If the Nanny has prior incidents on her driving record which has raised the insurance premium, it is not uncommon for the employer to request that the Nanny pay the difference in cost because of the unsafe driving points on her driving record. In the event of an accident while on duty, if the Nanny is at fault, it is reasonable that s/he should pay the deductible. It is not unusual for the employer to expect the Nanny to put gas in the car when it is used during off-duty hours. The employer may limit the amount of miles per week for personal use in order to conserve the life of the car for as many years as possible and to keep its value. If an employer wants you to use your own car to transport the children, etc., they should give you the current IRS mileage allowance and pay for the gas. Some employers will offer to purchase a car for the Nanny and then deduct an amount from the weekly salary to pay back the loan at no interest. In this instance, you should choose a car that you want to own.

Frequent Meetings

It is a good idea to plan to meet weekly to discuss what's going on and also just for the opportunity to talk to one another without the children. You will tend to know and like each other better because you have both taken the time to get to know one another. This is a relationship maintenance practice which is proof that the parties value the relationship and each other's role in it.

Speak Up When You Have Something On Your Mind

This cannot be emphasized enough. Each person has a responsibility to speak up anytime something needs to be discussed, otherwise resentment brews, burnout accelerates, and tempers can flare. Don't be afraid of hurting someone else's feelings. You are hurting the relationship by keeping your feelings to yourself and building resentment. Usually when someone says they don't want to hurt another person's feelings, they may really mean that they feel awkward, or uncomfortable discussing what ever is on their mind. *Keep in mind, those things that really bother us that we are reluctant to discuss, are usually the things that really need to be communicated for the sake of the relationship.*

Be On Time

This is an issue for both parents and Nanny. It is essential to call if you are going to be late for any reason. Not doing so suggests disrespect for the other person. This is an issue that comes up most frequently with parents who are running late. If this happens often, discuss it and try to build in some extra time at the end of the day. If possible ask to be compensated. To avoid discussion and simmer with anger because your plans were ruined, will erode the relationship. Bring it up in a non-threatening manner. Use the Process Recording form found in the Communication chapter.

Practice Random Acts Of Kindness

Go out of your way to do something thoughtful. Offer to stay with the children if they'd like to get away overnight. You might be amazed at the kind of chain reaction you can start. This is another form of "relationship maintenance" which strengthens the employer/employee relationship and builds up good feelings for those times when things become stressful as they sometimes will.

Termination Friction

When the Nanny has given notice and is leaving, friction can rear its ugly head even in the best of situations. For many people it is difficult to separate amicably. It seems that some of us need to get on each other's nerves as part of the ritual of leaving. This is a pattern that has been seen in hundreds of situations. It is probably easier to say good bye this way, however it's stressful and there are better ways to separate. The important thing is to know it happens, and to talk about it. Try to see the humor whenever you can. The Nanny may find that the things, or certain little habits her employer has always had, really start to annoy her. It also works the other way around for the parent/employer. Remember that this is a normal occurrence. Be aware of this dynamic and don't let it give you amnesia. You wouldn't be going through this if you didn't like each other.

Extending The Work Agreement

Advise parents to extend the work agreement at each six-month point, to extend the agreement for a year in advance. Parent/employers want continuity, which is very important, and would like to have a Nanny stay as long as possible in their employ. (Most agencies will not place a Nanny who cannot or will not guarantee a one-year minimum agreement). Therefore, your employer may approach you at the six month point of your first year, to ask if you would like to extend your agreement beyond the first year. This also provides a vehicle to plan ahead, to discuss ways to meet each others long term needs, changes, to ensure continuity for the child(ren).

Bonus & Salary Increases

Performance reviews in writing are encouraged as a basis for salary increases. Salary increases will vary depending on your review. Written reviews will also help to measure how you are meeting your goals, to settle possible conflicts, and will be good to have in your portfolio for the future. Bonuses may be given in lieu of a raise, especially if the employer wants to retain you for the long haul. Raising the Nanny's base salary could result in the family not being able to afford the Nanny.

Schedules

Your position should not be so cumbersome as to leave you no time for a social life. Everyone needs balance in their life and without it, will not function effectively. Employer's who do not recognize this should be avoided. The most common schedule is 8:00 am to 6:00 pm beyond that, any combination of hours can be negotiated depending on yours and the family's needs. Jobs that are advertised as having two to three hours off during the day supposedly enabling the employer the right to expect you to work the two or three hours beyond what is usually expected is unfair. The only exception to this is if you are attending classes during that off time, or have another responsibility. Even in these instances, however, if a child is ill, the Nanny will usually be expected to miss the class or the other responsibility in order to stay with the ill child. That is the standard expectation.

Errands While On Duty

As with any other kind of job, it is unprofessional to do your own errands on your employer's 'dime.' The unsupervised nature of this job lends itself to type of abuse. The employer expects to have all the time agreed upon spent on the specific needs of the child and the family. Resist any temptation to drop by the mall to look for something to wear out to dinner while you are on-duty. Don't be unfair to the employer.

Scheduling Vacations

The Nanny and the employer should mutually decide what the vacation schedule will be. It should never be the decision of one or the other alone. This might have been discussed during the interview and certain stipulations made as part of the job offer.

At-Home Parent

Some nannies will not even interview for a position where there is a parent at home during the day for valid reasons. It is usually much more difficult for the Nanny to form a bond with the child if she is competing with mom or dad because the child, (especially younger), tends to want to be with family members over the nanny. The parent must be sophisticated enough to understand the dynamic that occurs when two adults are in the home caring for the children, or even if the parent works in a separate office in the house. When interviewing for this kind of position, look for sensitivity on the part of the at-home parent to be willing to "back you up" by letting the children know that if Nanny said "no more cookies", that means *no more cookies*. The children cannot go to the at-home parent every time they want a decision that Nanny has made, overturned. It's vital to have your duties very clearly spelled out so that you know what you are responsible for, rather than waiting around for the at-home parent to tell you what she needs you to do next. You must discuss directly the need for the parent to back you up and vice versa. You need to discuss in depth how limits will be set for the children. In this situation, more than ever, discussion & agreement on rules, discipline & consistency is vital. Some parents understand how to successfully be at home and blend into the environment in a helpful way so as not to disrupt the routine. We know that in almost every situation, when another person enters room where two or more other people are interacting—the dynamic changes. A good example of this is when parents return after being at work all day and suddenly the preschooler who had been playing contentedly until then—has a major melt-down. Ask for references. Before accepting the position, ask the name of the Nanny that was previously employed in the position you are considering, and ask questions such as:

- Did the parent back up the Nanny? (with reference to Discipline)
- Did S/he end up doing more chores than child-care?
- What was it you liked or enjoyed the most?
- Did the Nanny ever feel undermined?
- Was the parent supportive of the Nanny?
- Were they helpful with the transition?
- Did you enjoy working with the family?
- Did you feel comfortable living and working within the home?
- Is the parent moody or irritable?
- Does the schedule remain intact, or does it frequently change? Was that a problem?
- "Is there anything you can tell me that will help me work better within the family?

Friends & Visits

As with any other job, your friends should never be at your workplace while you are on duty. Telephone conversations should be limited to confirming plans or arranging for a time to talk when you are off duty. Let your friends know that you take your job seriously. If you live-in, it is not appropriate to have many different dates come to the house to pick you up. You should meet elsewhere. Let your "significant other" know that you take your job seriously and handle your relationship in a responsible manner. Only a "significant other" should come to your employer's home if you live-in, but only with an agreement with the family. If you live out, it should never occur unless you are being picked up or dropped off. Bear in mind that some people are very territorial about their home and are not comfortable whatsoever with the idea of the nanny's friends, or even her family members being there when they are not. Always be considerate of this.

Food

Your employer will usually tell you what you can help yourself to as far as the food, snacks & drinks in the house. If they don't bring it up, be sure you do. If you live-out, just as with any job, you should expect to bring your own lunch, drinks and snacks, unless they have offered otherwise. It's disconcerting for a parent to go into the freezer for their favorite ice cream after a long day at the office only to find it almost gone. If you live-in it's not unusual for your employer to perhaps buy your brand of cereal, or a certain kind of bread for you. Ask directly if there are items they prefer you to leave intact. If you have the run of the kitchen and you have been told to help yourself, that generosity applies to you alone—not to a friend who stops in. When hosting playgroups in your employers home, ask if you can serve refreshments and discuss with your employer specifically what you will serve.

Housework

Housework as a major part of the responsibility should always be under a separate agreement with an amount of salary apportioned for that responsibility in order to clearly identify from the main responsibility of a Nanny. Should you find that it is too much and you wish to drop the housework from your duties, that portion of the salary can be dropped. Before agreeing to include housework with the child-care, be certain of the expectation, i.e., what duties are included (bathrooms, bedrooms, kitchen, whole house, etc.) and whether or not you are capable of handling all of it. Some employers do not recognize the time involved in heavy housework. If there is a child crawling around when you are trying to wash the kitchen floor, or a toddler disappearing up the stairs, your first responsibility is to the child and it might not be possible to complete the heavy housework. Plus, it is stressful to continually be interrupted which can be the case when combining child-care and housekeeping. Resentment could become an issue if the nanny feels like a maid, or that she is being taken advantage of.

Employers who seem to be squeezing every ounce of work from the nanny are sometimes the same parents that don't value the nanny's role in the development of their child. To avoid these pitfalls, both the Nanny and the employers must understand and agree to the duties involved from the beginning and negotiate any new responsibilities separately as they appear.

Working In A Stressful Environment

You have the right to work in a reasonably stress-free environment. In situations where there is 'tension' in the household, i.e., your employees arguing, cold wars, yelling or other behaviors, which may be uncomfortable for you. Consider approaching them to let them know that their behavior is a problem for you. This may encourage them to find better solutions for coping with their communication with each other. If an older child or another family member is creating 'tension' in your work setting, you must discuss this problem with the appropriate person. (Refer to the Chapter on 'Communication' for ways to discuss problems with your employer).

Telephone Use

If you live-in and there isn't a private line already, you may request your own phone line into the house that you should expect to pay for yourself. This will avoid friction such as, 'whose long distance calls are who's late night calls." "not having a phone available when you need one," etc. This is an option, to discuss with your potential employer. If you live-out, or live-in, excessive use of the telephone and or the Internet during the day is not a good idea, even if the children are sleeping. All of this activity is documented, therefore even if the family said to feel free to use either, it's likely they won't be thrilled to see your internet activity, or the telephone bill if it's more than 15 minutes a day.

Traveling With The Family

Accompanying the family on their vacation can be tricky. You are working, otherwise you may not have been invited to go along. If it is your vacation, you would be taking it away from your job, with your own family or friends. Therefore, if you are with the family, you are on-duty. Discuss, determine, and be absolutely certain what your schedule will be when you get there. The most nightmarish vacations have been when the Nanny went along expecting the fun on the Islands and finding herself in the hotel room watching a sleeping infant while everyone else is at the beach. Most employers will be sensitive and be flexible, but it is imperative to prearrange your schedule to avoid problems.

Differing Childcare Philosophies

Ideally, your employers and your own child rearing philosophies will not be radically different. However, an issue may present itself when the job is well underway. Parents will determine the style of limit-setting, what friends are allowed to visit, etc. On the other hand, should the Nanny become aware of the possibility of any abuse, physical, verbal, sexual, you should contact an abuse 'hot line' for advice (Refer to the Chapter on Ethics). Under all other circumstances, the nanny has the responsibility to follow the parent's directives for the care of their child and to follow their guidelines at all times.

Often, parents will request more from their nanny than what they, themselves, may do when caring for their children. For instance, a parent may ask that you never, ever turn the TV on and instead expect that you spend that time more creatively, and when the weekend comes you see that the children are mesmerized in front of the 'tube' while Mom and Dad are reading the newspaper. Keep in mind that they are paying you to provide the highest standard of care possible, and try to refrain from being judgmental. Many parents simply don't have the energy to be creative on the weekends. Being critical or forming judgments about how your employer manages his/her life or parenting issues, will almost never serve any worthwhile purpose. If this is a difficult area for you to accept, it may be wise to recognize this and deal with it before it becomes an issue on the job.

When To Tell The Children You Are Leaving

We advocate telling the children that you will be leaving at the time that you begin your job. Too many times, parents and nannies joke about "staying forever" and to children, this becomes their expectation. It is normal and healthy for anyone, in any job, to grow out of it, to want to seek different experiences. It doesn't mean that you care any less for the people you work for, its just a fact of life in our society. You should discuss with the parents when you will tell the children, but again, it is recommended that you do so sooner, rather than later. Ideally, prior to telling them, you and the parents should plan a time for you to return to visit so that when you tell the children you are leaving, you tell them at the same time when you will be back to see them. Keep in mind that children as young as six to eight months—although pre-verbal—understand what is said. Therefore, never let them overhear information that you are not ready to explain, or that could possibility cause the child to feel anxious.

Another reason why you should be authentic with them is that they WILL pick up on the little nuances, the subtle hints that you will undoubtedly let slip. For instance, you may not talk about what you will be doing on a particular child's birthday because you know you won't be there, etc. If a child knows something is up and no one is talking about it, it causes anxiety for them that is needless. When you tell them, keep it matter-of-fact. Talk about when you will be back to visit. Plan to write to one another. Perhaps the worst-case situation would be for the nanny to disappear without preparing the child, or saying goodbye. This can be very traumatic to a child and every effort should be made to prevent this from happening. Creating a gradual transition is vital to the well being of the child and this should be kept in mind, in all situations.

Professional Development

As with any profession, being aware of what is on the 'cutting edge' in the childcare field, is not only important to your career, but esteeming for you personally, as well. If there is a network available, join. Participate and contribute to the group, especially if you are working in a particularity isolated work environment—which is the case for most nannies. There are quite a few nanny chats/discussion groups on Yahoo and many are specific to certain states & cities.

Contact the Educational Institute for Professional Nannies, Inc. for information about their distance training program; Professional Nanny Online; 508-650-8889, or on the Internet at www.professionalnanny.com They have students from all over the United States, Canada, Europe & Asia and its very likely that you will meet other nannies from your area if you are part of PNO. On-going education is a respected and valuable asset. It's common knowledge that if two individuals are applying for the same job and one is educated in the field and the other isn't; the educated applicant will get the job 90% of the time. Moreover, they will also make a higher salary than the applicant without training. Another benefit of continuing education is greater confidence. Learning more about one's work is empowering and build's self-esteem. Once certified, you will be recognized for the knowledge and skills you possess, plus nannies changing positions find that they are more valuable to employers because of their certificate. Many employers, especially parents who are anxious to leave their children with someone while they work, have more peace of mind with an educated nanny & will offer salary increases once a nanny completes coursework. Some employers offer to cover the cost of class materials. If you continue your education, you may receive college credits for these courses depending upon the college you attend, your major and/or how many electives are required.

If you are in a position which provides time off during the day, you may also want to consider taking a class at a local college. This profession is one where there are many growth opportunities for those who are open to them.

CHAPTER TWO

Roles & Responsibilities

MAINTAINING A PROFESSIONAL ATTITUDE

Unlike most other jobs, the Nanny's role is complicated somewhat by the fact that she usually resides with her employer. Because of this, it is at times difficult to maintain a professional attitude. Even in situations where the Nanny does not live-in, she is, nevertheless, in her employer's home most of the day and exposed to all of the personal goings on that naturally occur in the privacy of anyone's home.

There are many pitfalls to this type of employer/employee relationship. The most common being that both sides become lax in the attention and time they give to the details of maintaining a professional relationship. It is hard to be objective with people we know well and whom we are fond of (and hopefully, all Nannies and families eventually feel this way about one another). Therefore, it is something that we must work on continuously throughout the course of our employment.

To start with a written contract will always preclude any job, and should include all of the areas discussed in the chapter on the Employment Agreement. It is also important to maintain an open line of communication right from the start. Therefore, you should suggest that both you and your employer(s) make a habit of meeting at least once of month to discuss whether or not each party's expectations are being met. Again, it is difficult to be objective, and so you need to make a real effort.

It is not unusual for employers to overuse the Nanny's services by arriving late more often than not or for a Nanny to slack off on maintaining some of her duties. Problems can arise if both sides can't feel comfortable speaking up anytime they feel they need to.

One of the greatest disadvantages to living with your employer and developing a friendly relationship, occurs when the Nanny allows her personal problems to overlap during her work hours. Moodiness or any other kind of inconsistency in attitude can ruin a good Nanny Family relationship faster than almost anything else. Therefore, maintaining a professional attitude includes keeping personal problems out of the workplace especially while on duty and preferably at all times.

NANNY AS ROLE MODEL

All parents will choose a Nanny based on their impression of her in the following ways:

❖ Is the Nanny articulate; i.e., good grammar, pleasing personality, polite, well groomed?

❖ Does the Nanny appear to be safety conscious? Capable of responding in an emergency? Kindhearted? Intelligent?

❖ Does the Nanny seem to have a good moral character (this is based mostly on credentials, but many parents rely on "gut" feelings).

In general, parents realize, at least subconsciously, that the Nanny will be an influence on their child. Because of this, the Professional Nanny, in carrying out her role, will always conduct herself in such a way as to be acceptable should the child mimic her (which the child eventually will). Many Nannies have reported that the children they care for will copy not only their most obvious behavior, i.e., language, but also mimic personal faults such as nail biting, junk food binging, etc. Children will also learn to copy attitudes, prejudices, hygiene habits, and other kinds of likes or dislikes, etc.

The professional Nanny's position as a "role model" cannot be emphasized enough. It is crucial that the Nanny recognize this responsibility and always conduct herself accordingly.

The following responsibilities are among those that Nannies perform. However, it is essential to understand that each family is different and has different needs; therefore, the family that you are employed by may require some, but not all, of the following. Some families may also have needs that we have not listed.

Responsibilities Required By Every Position

1. *Care of the Child or Children as the Priority:*
The Nanny should be more involved with child care than with any other responsibility (including activities, etc.). This includes feeding (i.e. meal planning, preparation, and cleanup), bathing, dressing, playing with and supervising, planning play. Some Nanny positions are in homes where children are school age. It is important to determine what priorities the employer has in these situations. You can expect that there may be a lot of evening and/or weekend care if child care is the priority. Also, be aware that in positions with school-age children, many employers may want a Nanny mainly to ensure a positive role model for their children, but may require a lot of home management duties.

You need to evaluate how satisfied you will be in this role. To enhance your professional role in these situations, investigate community resources, i.e., activities for the children, lessons, etc. in consultation with the parent(s).

2. *Participate in Planning~and Carrying Out an Appropriate Curriculum:*
This includes devising a "play plan" for each child, helping with homework and/or investigating community resources. You could discuss with the parents the possibility of organizing a play group with other Nannys.

Creative activities (see Curriculum Chapter) is the area most Nannys are the weakest in. It is important to concentrate on this area to be certain the children in your charge are spending their days meaningfully. This applies to infants as well as school-age children.

3. *Care of the Children's Environment:*

This includes the hygiene of their bathroom (even if it is shared), bedroom, including changing bed sheets once a week, or more often if needed (crib sheets once a day), vacuuming or sweeping weekly, unless a house cleaner comes. Laundry is best taken care of daily with infants, twice weekly with toddlers, and at least once weekly with older children. Keeping toys clean, removing broken or inappropriate toys (ones with small pieces that may have been given to an infant), and maintaining play areas and larger toys. Putting toys back where they belong with the child's assistance (age 3 or older) are all tasks you need to perform to care for a child's environment. Maintenance of other areas of the home used when caring for children; i.e., kitchen is also necessary. Therefore, the kitchen should be thoroughly cleaned after meals, including stove, sink, dishes, floor, etc.

Care of children's equipment, i.e., baby seats, high chairs, etc. is the Child Care Professional's responsibility as well. These should be thoroughly washed at least once a week and wiped off after each use.

General Responsibilities:

These general responsibilities apply to all Nannies:

- ✓ Conduct self ethically.
- ✓ Always follow parental guidelines.
- ✓ Prepare a daily log to keep parents informed.
- ✓ Maintain a safe, organized environment
- ✓ Maintain own living area and any area of home that is used when working and during time off.

✓ Make at least a one-year employment commitment.
✓ Be willing and eager to sign a contract which specifies the details of the position, the salary, and the benefits.

Responsibilities Required in Some But Not Every Position

✓ Drive children to and from school or activities.
✓ Accompany family on vacations and/or business travel.
✓ Plan and prepare menu, shop for food, cook.
✓ Remain on duty for extended periods of time while parents travel or while you accompany them out of town, or for other reasons.
✓ Perform heavy housework; i.e., ovens, windows, clean parents' room and bath; ~ this is only done under a separate agreement
✓ Shop for children's clothes.
✓ Run errands, i.e., dry cleaning drop off, etc.
✓ Work longer than a ten-hour day as a regular schedule.
✓ Work evenings, a few nights per week, or weekends.
✓ Participate in family activities; i.e., religious customs if (and sometimes when) the parents cannot be present.
✓ Other. There may be requests an employer may make that we have not listed.

ENHANCING PARENT-CHILD RELATIONSHIPS

As with most human service careers, the role of the Nanny is multi-faceted, depending on the needs of the people she is working with. Nevertheless, one of the most important responsibilities is the nanny's role in enhancing the parent-child relationship. This is one of the most significant ways in which a nanny distinguishes herself from other child caregivers.

In order for this to happen the nanny must value and gain satisfaction from "making a difference" in someone else's life. There are some people who go to their jobs & function well enough. They sometimes enjoy aspects of it, and other times they may watch the clock, waiting for the day to end. On the other hand there are people who gain a lot of personal or Job satisfaction from looking at their job from a much different perspective. They step back, look at the "big picture" and can see where a little extra kindness can make a difference. They look to see what they can do to help enhance the quality of the lives of the people they care and work for. This isn't to say that they don't have bad days, or that they always put themselves last. They have learned that it feels good to do a little extra to make life easier for the people around them. It's gratifying to know that their actions made a difference to someone else & they have made it a habit to think this way. Again its not because they are a "Pollyanna". They get something out of it that means more to them than a raise. They find that their personal self-esteem grows and their confidence in themselves keeps getting stronger. They in effect, do as much for themselves as they do for the people they are going out of their way for.

Examples of how this responsibility is realized is as follows:

EXAMPLE 1:

You notice that each day upon Mrs. Low's arrival from work, her two children, ages 3 and 5 surround her, simultaneously asking questions, telling about their day, sometimes complaining, all before she has had an opportunity to relax. You realize that she has a stressful job. Furthermore, you are sensitive to the fact that it is difficult to leave one responsibility (her office) to enter directly into another (caring for her children). As a result, you ask her if she would like you to plan an activity for the children either at home, or away from home during the same time she usually returns from work to give her an opportunity to catch her breath before spending time with the children.

EXAMPLE 2:

You notice that Jimmy, age 4, "acts out" as soon as his father appears, whining, complaining, and arguing with everyone. You suspect that this is attention-seeking behavior directed at his father. You could suggest to your employer that arranging a special time for just the two of them (even for as little as five minutes, if time is a problem) may help reduce this "acting-out." Suggest an activity for them; i.e., provide books, a game, or specific ideas about what keeps Jimmy happily occupied. If Jimmy can count on having this time with his dad and at the same time, you organize an activity to keep him stimulated while his dad is getting home at the end of the day, things would likely go a lot more smoothly.

EXAMPLE 3:

Mr. and Mrs. Danforth, your employers, are sometimes involved in discussion when you enter the room, at the end of the day with their two-year old,. Today it is obvious that they are talking about something important. Although you are no longer on duty, you tell their two-year-old that the two of you should go down to the playroom and check out the new computer game you got at the library. This gives her employer's some time to talk privately without interruption

EXAMPLE 4:

Mrs. Woodworth, your employer, has just returned home from the hospital with her newborn. Although she denies it, she appears tired, worn out, and is irritable. She is also breast-feeding and getting up every few hours around the clock. You suggest that she consider expressing breast milk so you can take care of the night feedings or that she consider giving formula every other night so she can get a full night's rest.

CHAPTER THREE

Professional Nanny Process

Organizing Your Time

The Professional Nanny Process is modeled after the Nursing Process in that it is a tool to use to:

Assess; what's needed in every area
Plan; how to carry out all of your responsibilities
Implement: the plan, including writing it down, and
Evaluate, it's effectiveness on a regular basis

Priorities;

In the order of priority, the Nanny starts with:

Personal Care of each child followed by,
Children's Activities and then,
Home Hygiene & Management duties

The nanny then describes each function, in each area specifically, in order to maximize her understanding of the full scope of her duties, organize her time efficiently, and then evaluate along with the employer the overall content, and execution of the nanny's work.

The documented Professional Nanny Process form is a complicated task, requiring time and energy. Only a nanny who truly functions as a professional is capable of completing a Professional Nanny Process including a meaningful evaluation of how time is spent. However time consuming and difficult a well done Professional Nanny Process is, the benefits are well worth it.

Employers have made comments such as:

"It's a great feeling to know that the person who cares for the children is so serious about her work".

"I feel so secure with our nanny, she really carries out and documents her duties better than some nurses I've known."

"The Grid is there along with full descriptions which have been helpful not only to me, but babysitters I've hired in the evening."

"When I saw the effort that our nanny put into going over every aspect of her job, we knew this person was exactly what we've needed in our hectic household."

"Now my husband can see in black and white the work that's involved in properly caring for children."

"Every nanny should do this. It's tangible proof that she's involved in her profession and takes pride in it. We are very fortunate to have such a conscientious person caring for our child.

Nanny's have said:

"I worked on a holiday for another nanny and felt so confident since everything was written down so specifically in her Professional Nanny binder."

"The Professional Nanny Process got me my raise; my employer could really see what I was doing with my time."

"My employer reduced some of my workload when I showed her my Professional Nanny Process Grid along with the full explanations—it was obvious that there were just not enough hours in the day."

"After evaluating my Professional Nanny Process Grid, I saw that I had a lot of time on Mondays and Thursday, whereas Wednesdays were just too hectic. I revised my schedule and things go a lot more smoothly. I had not even realized how lopsided my schedule was until I wrote it all out and looked at it!"

"Having a written schedule has been very helpful in getting me organized. I've never been so organized."

PURPOSE

1. To enable the Nanny to integrate the theoretical and practical components of her training in an organized, systematic way to facilitate assessment and evaluation of both the responsibilities required by her position and her performance.
2. To enhance the cognitive, emotional, and social development of each child in her charge.
3. To enhance the organized management of the home.
4. To enhance the consistency and continuity of care provided to children from parent and Nanny.
5. To also provide the means to achieve a smooth transition between caregivers in the nanny's absence.

Before you begin, keep the following points of emphasis in mind.

POINTS OF EMPHASIS

- The Professional Nanny Process, once completed is not "cast in stone," deviation from the usual schedule will occur and as long as it is not a chronic deviation that renders the whole written routine null and void, don't be concerned. Working with children requires that we adjust our priorities regularly.

- A very important part of the Professional Nanny Process is the actual thinking through and the writing of it. This will help us understand our responsibilities more fully and provide documented evidence that we are fully committed and understand our responsibilities.
- The Professional Nanny Process must be revised every three months when caring for an infant and toddler up to the age of two. After that, revise only as needed.
- As you learn new or better ways of doing things, change the information in your Professional Nanny Process and make a note in your daily log that a change was made.
- A meaningful Professional Nanny Process can not be written until a nanny has been in a position for at least a month. It takes at least that long to have a good grasp of the depth and breadth of your responsibilities.
- Be mindful that young children are extremely ritualistic. They prefer routine and will become confused if the routine is always changing. Stating what routines you follow and incorporating, as appropriate the routines that were in place prior to your arrival shows intelligence and sensitivity.

THE PROFESSIONAL NANNY PROCESS CHECKLIST

The Professional Nanny Process includes three major areas:

1) PERSONAL CARE
2) ACTIVITIES
3) HOME HYGIENE AND MANAGEMENT

Complete one checklist for each child, (Starting with the oldest child first) Circle all tasks that the Nanny is responsible for.

CHILD'S NAME: _____ AGE_____

1) List all child's personal care needs

2) List all child's activities (refer to your child's curriculum)

3) List all Home Hygiene & Management duties

PART 1: CHILD CARE (PERSONAL CARE) WORKSHEETS: Duties and Detail

1) List and number each child care responsibility, in each area; *Personal Care*, i.e., bathing, grooming, feeding, dressing. *Activities*; i.e. the library, the park, pet store & Home Hygiene & Management, i.e. grocery shopping, meal prep, keeping babies room clean & neat
2) Describe the responsibility FULLY. Include detail (a caregiver filling in for you will know exactly how to proceed after reading your FULL DESCRIPTIONS of each responsibility).
3) State the time approximate allocation for each (how long does each responsibility take).
4) State the preferred time to provide this care, i.e., mornings, or afternoons, etc.

WORKSHEET 1—PERSONAL CARE

EXAMPLE OF WHAT YOUR DUTIES MAY BE (Every position is different)

1. Get children up in the morning
2. Change diapers
3. Use potty chairs, clean potty, wash hands
4. Dress
5. Supervise unstructured play
6. Prepare breakfast, serve, feed as necessary
7. Wash hands, brush teeth, wash face, comb hair
8. Check nails, clean as necessary
9. Unstructured play (Nanny organizes kitchen)
10. Activity—Structured
11. Change diapers
12. Potty, wash hands

13. Snack/bottle
14. Baby down for a nap
15. Activity—Structured
16. Activity—unstructured (Nanny chores)
17. Baby up, change diapers, potty, wash hands
18. Prepare lunch, serve, feed as necessary
19. Prepare bath, bath (wash hair, toe nails, ears, blow hair dry/style, dress)
20. Structured Activity (read, study)
21. Nap (both children)
22. Get children up
23. Change diapers, potty, wash hands
24. Structured activities

WORKSHEET 2—CHILDREN'S ACTIVITIES

Worksheets—Examples of Activities and Duties

1. List and number each activity, i.e. Playgroup, reading, Gymboree and uninstructed play
2. Describe the activity FULLY. Include details and the location of the activity. (Directions may be necessary)
3. State the time allocation for each activity (can be flexible)
4. State the preferred time for the activity, or exact time. (can be flexible)

EXAMPLES OF DUTIES RELATED TO ACTIVITIES

Library
Reading stories
Music (listening)
Music(lessons)
Playgroup:
Formal
Informal

Gymboree
Make holiday cards
Swimming & lessons
Fishing in lake
Sledding (wintertime)
Helping with housework
Helping bath the baby (doll)
Music and dance
Play house/dress up
Help build a model
Play catch
Field trips
After school activities, i.e. sports, etc.

EXAMPLES OF TIME ALLOCATION/PREFERRED TIME

(Example) 1-1/2 hours each day Tuesday & Thursday. Directions, where library card is kept etc., books he/she likes can be found…
(Example) The cassette player is kept…The tapes are kept…he/she likes to tell stories about books (from library) while he/she is being taped. Then we play the story back. Ask questions about the story as he/she tells it to draw him out more…" (Good gift for Mom & Dad or faraway relative.)
(Example) Whenever Child seems moody or if there is tension or stress in the house, we draw pictures of each other and talk about the picture i.e., Child is angry or happy—I just let him talk about how he/she feels without being judgmental or I'll tell him how I feel etc.

OTHER *(please list)*

WORKSHEET 3: HOME MANAGEMENT

1. List and number each home management duty, i.e., laundry, kitchen hygiene, meal preparation etc.
2. Describe the data FULLY. Include detail. State location of necessary supplies, and what specifically they are.
3. State the time allocation for each.
4. State the preferred time to start and complete each duty.

Examples of Home Hygiene & Management Duties

Meal planning
Meal preparation all
Breakfast (only)
Lunch (only)
Dinner
Meal clean-up all
Breakfast (only)
Lunch (only)
Dinner (only)
Dishes & pans
Floor; Sweep and mop floor after each meal.

Table top
Chairs/high chairs
Counter tops; wipe off counter tops, appliance tops, etc. after each meal.

Child's bedroom/linen
Child's bathroom
Toy hygiene Clean all toys. Don't allow water to get trapped inside toys with holes
Rotate toys.

Pick up children's toys in yard, porches and deck. Have preschool aged & older children help

Laundry (separate from all other laundry) each sky fold, put away neatly, iron as necessary.

Change crib sheets daily. State where sheets are kept.
Change single bed sheets twice a week.
Organize children's bedrooms daily.
- drawers
- closets
- bookcases
- toy box

Vacuum children's rooms as needed, (in addition to housekeeper.)

Wash children's equipment twice daily i.e. high chairs, bed rails (once weekly) and crib rails, crib and bed toys.
Clean tub before use and wipe out often.
Maintain shopping list (post on refrigerator).

Shop for groceries

EXAMPLE

COMPLETED
PROFESSIONAL NANNY PROCESS
WORKSHEETS

SECTION 1—PERSONAL CARE

Nutrition

Meals and Snacks—Child and Child

Specify Age

Breakfast between 8 am–9 am
Juice every morning

MENU: Cheerios & whole wheat toast
          Scrambled eggs & wheat toast
          French toast
          Banana on toast

SNACK between 10 am–10:30 am
Juice and Select: Piece of fruit
                  Carrot
                  Celery stick
                  Raisins

LUNCH between 11:45 am–12:30

MENU: Fish sticks & French fries
          Peanut butter & jelly

Soup & crackers
Sliced chicken/turkey/ham with tomato (no bread)

SNACK between 2 pm–2:15
See 10 am snack menu
Child only (Child in school)

SNACK between 4:15–4:30
See 10 am snack menu

GENERAL POINTS OF EMPHASIS

- Keep juice pitcher in refrigerator filled at all times with juice
- Never offer candy, we eat fruit instead (holidays, etc. only)
- Never use food as a "surprise" or reward
- Child may have white bread with sandwiches only, whole wheat or bran for toast or French toast in the morning.

SUPPER between 5 pm–5:30 pm
MENU and directions
A) *Chicken cutlets, boiled potatoes, vegetable, salad*
   Cook chicken according to directions on package wash potatoes with green vegetable brush, (don't peel) cut in 2" x 2" pieces salad, wash lettuce, break by hand, (restaurant size pieces), add tomatoes, celery, cracker barrel cheese (cut into cubes) Vegetable, peas/corn/green beans.
B) *Baked ham, baked potatoes, vegetable, salad*
   Place ham on flat baking sheet, after covering pan with tin foil bake in lower oven at 350 for 40 minutes wash potatoes with green vegetable brush, stab, place in microwave for 10 minutes (one for each adult, children will share one) vegetable and salad, see above.
C) *Pork chops (thin cut) shells, salad*
   After defrosting pork, shake & bake according to directions on package. Prepare "Prince" brand shells according to directions on box, salad as above.

D) *Fish fillet, rice, salad*
Prepare fish and rice according to instructions vegetable and salad as above

E) *Roast beef, mashed potatoes, vegetable, salad*
After defrosting beef, place on baking rack inside baking pan w/2" sides sprinkle with garlic and onion powder (not salt) Bake in lower oven for one hour at 350 Peel potatoes, cut in small pieces, boil until fork can easily be inserted, drain, mash adding 1/4 stick butter and a tablespoon milk, vegetable and salad as above.

F) *Broiled chicken, macaroni and cheese, vegetable*
After defrosting chicken breasts, place on baking rack inside baking pan (as above) sprinkle garlic and onion powder, place in top broiler for seven minutes on high, then over, sprinkle garlic and onion powder, place in top broiler for seven minutes on high, then turn to low setting for five minutes, turn over, sprinkle with spices again, cook for seven minutes on high setting again then down to low setting for five more minutes. Prepare macaroni and cheese according to directions vegetable and salad as above. Please alter spices and seasonings according to the child's taste and the parents guidelines.

POINTS OF EMPHASIS

- Ask your child if he/she needs to go to the bathroom before meals.
- Serve eggs no more than once a week.
- Dilute Child's juice 1/4 strength water
- NEVER add sugar to cereal. Limit jelly on toast (spread thinly.) Limit syrup on French toast
- No cookies or Popsicles in morning
- Child MUST be watched the entire time when he/she is eating celery or carrots. No raisins, popcorn, or hard candy.
- Fruit MUST be cut in very small pieces
- Ask Child if he/she needs bathroom

- No salt added to any food (don't let the children see you add it to yours!).
- Be enthusiastic about how GOOD the meal is!
- Bake the French fries, don't fry.
- If you are drinking soft drinks, put it in a non-see-thru cup
- Don't eat any kind of "junk" food in front of your child.

Kitchen/General

- Keep gate at top of basement stairs closed securely
- Your child should always be in eyesight
- Keep screen door locked
- Never leave children alone when they are eating (choking!)
- Food and drinks in kitchen only
- All pan handles turned in, so they can't be grabbed!
- Child should not be in walker: (walker not recommended)
  - ✓ You are putting hot food in/out of oven
  - ✓ You are carrying anything hot from the stove to sink or table
  - ✓ oven is on—door gets hot!
  - ✓ You are loading/unloading dishwasher
  - ✓ You are not in the room with him
- Don't leave children alone unsupervised, Child could hurt Child
- Child may go outside alone only when ALL gates are secured, including gates to driveway, and only when you are in kitchen, checking him every few minutes

BATHING ROUTINE

Tell Child beforehand that he/she will be taking a bath in "Two Minutes". Ask Child if he/she needs to use the "Potty" before he/she gets into the tub. Check tub to be sure it's clean, no hairs, etc. wipe out with dry paper towel. Fill tub 1/4 full, with tepid water. Be sure all needed items are in bathroom within reach, large towel, baby shampoo, plastic bowl, wash cloth, etc.

Undress in bathroom, and into tub, (when bathing Two or more children, bathe the youngest child first). Rinse hair with water, place dime size amount of shampoo on head, lather, and rinse (about three times), wipe eyes if necessary although the water doesn't bother either of them usually. However, try to avoid getting it in their eyes as much as possible. Use the baby shampoo to wash everywhere—don't put regular bar soap in tub, they may touch it then wipe their eyes which will sting! Wash with cloth according to proper bathing techniques. When taking Child out of tub, stand him on the mat in front of you, and then wrap him in the towel—Never let go of him, even for a second! Make sure both Child and Child's feet are on mat/rug, NOT floor when they get out of the tub, tile on floor is slippery!!! Carry to bench in kitchen, dry off, and dress in PJ's (use powder only if rash is present.)

POINTS OF EMPHASIS

- Child's bath only lasts about five minutes. Child likes to stay in tub and play with bath toys; he/she can play in tub for about 15 minutes. Child won't want to take his bath, just tell him "It's time!" and once he/she's in he/she won't want to get out! Tell him you'll be going to his room to play a TERRIFIC game, after he/she's in his PJ's.
- Child's skin is very sensitive, be sure bath water is tepid, temperatures that are comfortable for adults can burn babies!
- Be sure water doesn't cool off before bath is completed, move child away from faucet, and add hot water, then move water in tub with your hand to spread hot water.
- NEVER, NEVER leave Child alone in tub OR alone with Child in tub, always keep one hand on Child when he/she's in the water, he/she could lean over and fall under very easily!

- If the phone or the doorbell rings while you're bathing Child, or if you need to check on Child, PICK UP Child, wrap him in a towel and take him with you.
- Change crib sheet every day after bath.

Grooming

Faces will always be clean, (use paper towel with water to wipe off faces and hands)

Hair will always be neat looking—run the brush under warm water and use if Child's hair is "mussed" or full of static.

Child's hair care before going to school:

- Gather equipment; round brush, yellow brush, blow dryer
- Have him sit on stool in kitchen
- Wet yellow brush by running it under faucet, run through hair, especially ends
- Using round brush, and blow dryer, curl ends under
- Be careful not to let hot air blow too close to his skin
- Child's hair is self-styling! (what hair he/she has)

Always be sure nails are clean! Trim nails after bath, fingers and toes

Check ears for wax/dirt after bath, clean with a damp cloth and your little finger, NEVER insert Q-tips!!

Child must be reminded to wash his hands after using the potty—each time.

Child needs help brushing his teeth, after breakfast and before his bath

- You brush them first, as demonstrated
- He/she can brush them for a little while
- Try to make it FUN, don't nag

Sleep Routines

Wake both children up at the predetermined time the parents have established, if they are sleeping.

Child sometimes wants to stay in bed (Children sometimes stay up later if parents haven't seen their children all day). If the Child doesn't want to get up, try bringing the Child whose awake into the other Child's room and play with him/her on the floor—make lots of noise, open the curtains and let him/her know what a great time he/she's missing! This may work for small children, but as the children get older it becomes more difficult. Experiment with different things, but do not use bribery, candy, sweets etc, as this will create another problem.

Before going down stairs, choose pants, top, underwear, and socks for Child from his closet. Both children shall be dressed before going down stairs.

Child's NAP begins between 1:30–2 pm (3 hours).

Try to keep Child up in the morning if at all possible, if he/she needs a nap, it should not be longer than one hour.

Anytime Child is home during Child's nap, A child gate should be used, leading to main hall so that Child can't get in his room and hop on the crib with him! (sometimes when Child is supposed to be resting or watching a video, he/she creeps up to Child's room).

Always be sure intercom is ON.

Specific Routine

- Lay child down on his back in the crib.
- Give him his pacifier and blanket.
- Cover him with his quilt.
- Turn on his musical Teddy, "kiss" him around the shoulders and neck, while you smack your lips and make kissing sounds (this really makes him laugh!!)
- Pull down shades.
- Say "Have a nice nap" and walk out and close the door.

Child should NEVER take a bottle to bed, and he/she only uses his pacifier and blanket in bed, they are always left in the crib. He/she will never go right to sleep, he/she rarely cries. If he/she does, go back in and check him, if he/she's fine, tell him it's time to go to sleep and leave.

DRESSING GUIDELINES

Clothes should always:

1) Match
2) Be wrinkle free
3) Be unstained
4) Be clean, change during the day if necessary
5) Fit well
6) Be weather appropriate

POINTS OF EMPHASIS

- Laundry is best done daily while Child is in school and Child is napping.
- Be sure to fold and put away clean laundry right away so it won't wrinkle, and so Child won't drag it around the kitchen.
- Child's button-down shirts are hung in his closet.
- Child's clothes are kept in oak dresser in kitchen.
- In chilly weather dress children in layers, i.e. undershirt, shirt, sweater, then a coat before going outside.
- Always put hats on before going out when temperature is below 50 degrees.

SECTION 2—ACTIVITIES

Unstructured every day morning activities: (various ages)

1. Sit Child on the floor with some toys, TALK ABOUT EVERY-THING THAT'S GOING ON

2. Give him different toys or safe kitchen utensils (wooden spoon, etc.) to play with, he/she gets bored after playing with the same toy after a while. Always rotate toys.
3. Ask Child if he/she'd like to see how fast he/she can dress all by himself, or Ask him if he/she'd like to watch Sesame St.
4. Turn on nursery rhyme tape or Raffe tape on bakers rack in kitchen and ask Child to sing-a-long with you.
5. Allow your child to watch an age-appropriate video & tell you all about it afterward (use a recorder to record the child telling the story back to you. This is a great gift for a parent)

POINTS OF EMPHASIS

- Be sure there is nothing on floor around Child that he/she could put in his mouth, i.e. dirt, etc. or small toys belonging to Child that he/she could choke on.
- Keep dining room door and back door shut so Child can't get out of the kitchen.
- Keep Child away from bench in kitchen, he/she has caught his fingers between the underside of the bench.
- Keep screen door locked so Child can't slip out and also so Child won't fall out should the latch not be secure.
- Keep chairs pushed in under the table so Child won't get under the table when he/she's in (he/she has stood up under the table and banged his head).
- Any away from home activities must be cleared with me first, and planned at least a day in advance.
- Only child-oriented activities away from home. Children do not enjoy long shopping trips, nor do they enjoy lengthy visits in non-child proofed homes.
- Playgroup—Every Wednesday morning 9:00 am, our house.

Guidelines

1. Children are not allowed in dining, or living rooms, kitchen only
2. No running is allowed inside the house.
3. Climbing stairs is not allowed.
4. Nanny will always be present outside anytime a child is outside, either on the deck or in the yard.
5. ALWAYS keep front driveway gate closed during playgroup.
6. Keep gate on deck locked, and gate between main house and carriage house.
7. Lock gate at top of basement stairs and also close the door (to prevent falls in case one of the children opens the door).
8. If necessary, remind other Nannies here at playgroup that they are responsible for keeping a close eye on their children.

Child's Play Plan (three and a half years old)

*   Put a piece of paper in a typewriter and let the Child type. You can type his name and address first, and ask him to see if he/she can copy it.
*   Put a chair in front of the kitchen sink, wrap a towel around Child, and let him give his "baby" a bath. he/she uses baby shampoo, and a paper towel.
*   Read him a story and ask him to tell you about the story afterwards. Using the cassette player (kept in the hall closet across from the bathroom), record him telling you the story, and then play it back.
*   Put on the nursery rhyme tape and show him how to "Act Out" the story, with each of you as one of the characters, (he/she likes to pretend to be the "big bad wolf" in the story of the "Three Little Pigs."
*   Have a sing-a-long, dance-a-long with the Raffe tape.
*   Ask him/her to draw a picture of himself when he/she's happy (sad, angry), and tell you about it, i.e. "Draw me a picture of happy

Child, why is Child happy?" Then you can draw a picture of yourself, giving examples of what makes you feel happy, sad, or angry.

- Make some broken-line letters, so he/she can trace them.
- Ask him/her to help you sweep the kitchen floor, and vacuum the other floors. he/she also enjoys helping fold laundry, make beds, (unmake beds), arranging his bookshelf in alphabetical order, and giving his plastic toys a bath (which they need now and then!).
- Play baseball out in the yard. His red plastic bat is in the back hall closet along with his white plastic ball.
- Bake muffins. Child will do a good job mixing the ingredients, after you put them in a bowl. Have him kneel in his chair at the table while mixing. He/she can also do well putting the batter into the cupcake pan liners, show him where on the box it tells how long to bake them, and then ask him to set the timer for that long.
- Call the library and reserve the computer (you have to do it that morning, so call early), walk to the library leaving about ten minutes before the time of your reservation. Child is familiar with how the computer works. Directions to the library are in the phone book on the counter, along with the library card. Child will play on the floor next to the computer, they have toys there for Child to play with.

Child's Play Plan (twelve months old)

- Have Child watch as you and the Child play the nursery rhyme tape and act out the story.
- Open a bottom cabinet door filled with Tupperware or other plastic bowls and let the child play with them pulling them out and playing with them. Put the radio on and pick him up and dance while holding him.
- Read him a story animating it by changing your voice for each character.

- Take him for a walk around the house, letting him stop each time he/she wants to check something out a little closer, try helping him up the stairs.
- At the end of every month remove some of his toys from the bottom of the Baker's rack, and replace with some of the toys in his bedroom closet. Let him pick out the ones he/she'd like from his closet.
- Walk to the playground and play on the swings.
- Let one of the cats in the house, and let Child pet it. Show him how to per "easy," demonstrate "hard" and "easy" by using the floor.
- Go out to lunch (when older brother is in school) at the "Deli" at the Framingham Mall, then visit the "Doctors" pet store. He/she loves to watch the fish, and look at the birds. Tell him about the birds and fish, name their colors, etc..

SECTION 3—HOME HYGIENE AND MANAGEMENT

Kitchen

Sweep kitchen floor and hall floors (between bathroom and kitchen and hall outside back door) a few times each day as needed. Use small hand held vacuum instead of a dust pan.

When trash is full, pull out green plastic bag, empty the bathroom trash into it, tie tightly and put in basement, (right side of basement, inside door at bottom of stairs). The trash can liners are kept in the cabinet above the cat food, (next to the back door).

POINTS OF EMPHASIS

- After handling trash, (soiled diapers too) remember to wash hands!!
- Make sure dishes are dry before putting them away.
- Check all pans (inside and out) and cutlery again before putting them away to be sure ALL grease, food particles, etc. are thoroughly removed.

- Wipe off stove front, and fronts of all appliances everyday, at the end of the day (to remove spilled food, etc.)
- Thoroughly clean Child's high chair, sassy seat (seat that attaches to kitchen table), edges of table that face Child and Child when they sit at the table, and check table legs and chairs for food and drink spills.
- Mop floor around and under table after each meal (crawlers will put anything in their mouths—this is a health & hygiene task, not housework)
- Wipe off sink in back of and around faucet after using the sink.
- Remember to wipe under small appliances when wiping off counter, after   preparing food.
- Always wash your hands before preparing food.
- Maintain ongoing grocery list, adding to it daily as needed.

Children's Bathroom

✓ Check toilet after Child uses it(sometimes he/she misses!), wipe off if necessary, also check base of toilet and floor, (wash hands).
✓ Rinse out sink after Child brushes his teeth.
✓ Check tub and wipe out before baths each day.
✓ Once a week, use comet and paper towels thoroughly clean all bathroom surfaces and fixtures. Follow instructions on bottle of toilet bowl cleaner, before cleaning toilet. (This is done in ADDI-TION to the bathroom hygiene that the bimonthly cleaning service does.)
✓ Towels hanging in bathroom are for "Looks," not for use as bath towels. Don't let Child wipe his face on them, especially if he/she has toothpaste on his face. They can be used for wiping hands after washing them.

Laundry

- It is done every day when possible.
- Child and Child's worn clothes go into the yellow hamper in the corner of the kitchen.

- Dishtowels, sponges, towels and any adult laundry should be put in the hamper at the bottom of the basement stairs.
- Run washer only when you are working in the kitchen, so you can hear washer if it becomes unbalanced (it has a habit of "jumping" should clothes be loaded unevenly, and we are concerned that the hoses may be ripped from the wall!)
- Load washer evenly, and don't wash heavy items with light items since this may increase the likelihood of the washer becoming unbalanced.
- Use only cold water, even with whites.
- Use the spray cleaner (which is kept on top of shelf next to washer and dryer) on stains before putting the stained item in the washer.

Child's Room

- Every afternoon, have Child help put his toys away, and organize his bookcase.
- Child will sweep the floor three times a week, and use the hand-held vacuum (instead of a dust pan), while you supervise and assist him.
- Ask him to help you make his bed.
- Twice a week, change the linens on his bed, the sheets for his bed are kept in his closet on the third shelf, on the left. They match the bed-spread.
- The crib sheet will be changed daily after his bath, sheets are kept in his left top dresser drawer.
- His pacifier should be washed in hot soapy water and rinsed thoroughly everyday
- His pacifier, small blanket, and yellow musical teddy should stay in the crib.
- His three bears sit on the rocking chair.
- The spread on the single bed in his room should be straightened out so that it looks neat after the children have played on it.

SAMPLE WEEKLY SCHEDULE					
	Monday	Tuesday	Wednesday	Thursday	Friday
8:00 am	Children up Breakfast (see menus) Dress	Same	Same	Same	Same
9:00 am	Unstructured play Kitchen clean up	Same	Same	Same	Same
9:30–11:00 am	Activity/Library (snack 10 am menus)	Playground	Playground	Playground	Library
11:30 am	Unstructured play Prepare lunch (see menus)	Same	Same	Same	Same
12:00 pm	Lunch	Same	Same	Same	Same
12:30 pm	Child ready/school Child unstructured play	Same	Same	Same	Same
12:50 pm	To school	Same	Same	Same	Same
1:15 pm	Bathe Child	Same	Same	Same	Same
1:45 pm	Story & Bottle for Child	Same	Same	Same	Same
2:00 pm	Child's nap (3 hrs) Home hygiene (see list) Prepare supper (see menus)	Same	Same	Same	Same
3:50 pm	Pick up Child	Same	Same	Same	Same
4:15 pm	Child's bath/PJ's (light snack)	Same	Same	Same	Same
4:30 pm	Child/video Prepare supper	Same	Same	Same	Same
5:00 pm	Child up/change into PJ's	Same	Same	Same	Same
5:30 pm	To living room/music	Same	Same	Same	Same

PROFESSIONAL NANNY PROCESS
EVALUATION

1) Child Care

   a) Is my detail section clear and concise?
   b) Am I practicing aseptic technique?
   c) Is my schedule organized or is it rushed?
   d) Do the children always look clean and neat? (other than when involved in play)?
   e) Are the children's nails clean and clipped at all times?
   f) Is hair clean and well groomed?
   g) Are meal times organized and relaxed most of the time?
   h) Is the bath time routine absolutely safe?
   i) What can I do to be more thorough?

2) Activities

   a) Is each detail thorough and concise?
   b) Am I providing at least one outdoor(or out of house) activity each day?
   c) Are the activities stimulating enough, over stimulating?
   d) Do the activities usually challenge the child or is boredom evident?
   e) Is there a variety of activities for the various growth and development needs of each child—physical, mental, emotional and social?
   f) Is there a balance between structured and unstructured activities?
   g) Have you planned cultural activities along with those that develop social skills?
   h) Make a list of new activities that can be implemented for the next stage of development.
   i) Are all activities age appropriate?

3) Home Management

   a) Are home management duties scheduled during nap/unstructured play/creative play times?

   b) Is there sufficient time to complete each duty as scheduled?

   c) Is there time to practice "Aseptic" technique whenever needed?

   d) Is the environment clean and orderly?

   e) Are children's toys and equipment clean and safe?

   f) Have all changes been noted in the log book?

CHAPTER FOUR

Communication

ACTIVE LISTENING

When we talk to someone who is a good listener and listens without judgment, we feel heard and understood. Sometimes we do not express our feelings to people whose reactions we fear. We, adults as well as children, fear hurt, rejection, criticism, doubt, and being wrong. Who are the people we go to for advice? Usually, we do not go to the hard practical ones who tell us exactly what to do, but instead we go to the listeners. Those who are kind, not censoring, not bossy and listen with an open heart. And by pouring out your problems to them, you then know what to do about your problems yourself. Creative listeners help us come up with your own answers.

There are many barriers to activate listening:

- Fear of criticism
- Leftover feelings; still reacting to a situation that previously happened.
- Misidentification or confusion; The person reminding you of someone else and reacting to that other person.
- Preoccupied with what you want to say.

A primary goal of the Nanny is to develop effective communication skills. The use of clear and honest dialogue is key to positive interaction with both parents and children. Expressing emotions simply and speaking from the heart allows for greater understanding and clear agreements. By staying calm and centered, the Nanny can approach problems with positive expectancy and learn from the challenges. Creating clear agreements and rules that everyone understands and feels good about involves doing what you say, and saying what you mean each day.

❖ Use "I feel" statements (I feel sad) instead of "you" statements (You made me sad).

❖ Speakers which start statements with "I feel" communicate assertively, honestly and directly.

❖ So much of communication is non-verbal. Be aware of what your body says and how it listens. Establish and maintain eye contact. If possible, be on the same eye level (physical equality). When listening, sit in a relaxed, receptive way.

❖ Communicate through love. When a child says "I want a horse," instead of saying "A horse is too expensive." Find out more about the wish. Learn what having a horse would do for the child. Ask questions like "what would it feel like if you had a horse?"

❖ We were given two ears with which to listen. Perhaps this means that we are meant to listen twice as much as we speak.

❖ We have the power to understand others. We have the power to accept others as they are and love them. We can do this best when we first understand ourselves and accept and love ourselves.

❖ Reconsider the use of absolutes, like "always" and "never" and instead use words which more accurately describe your experience. Instead of "I always get a speeding ticket, "use "I have, from time to time in my life, received a speeding ticket."

AWARENESS SKILLS

In your role as a Nanny there are number of awareness skills you will need to refine to enhance your communication skills. They are, for example:

- Listening
- Watching/reading body language
- Information processing, i.e., thinking objectively about what is being communicated, asking questions to clarify uncertainties.
- Decision making i.e., determining how you will respond, what your role will be, active, passive.
- Role taking i.e., following through on your role by using open ended questions or offering alternatives, etc.
- Problem solving i.e., identifying the feelings associated with the subject, putting them into perspective.

Where Is The Person Coming From?

Whether communicating with an employer, friend or relative, it is important for each participant to determine ahead of time what is the goal of the interaction, what are the ways to achieve this goal, and how to influence either the behavior or the mind of the other participant. In many situations, identifying the feelings behind the words is a more helpful strategy, than simply conversing about the matter at hand, since some conversations/interactions do not have a useful goal other than "acting out" or letting off steam. It is also important that you are aware of the social context of the communication. You should also realize that in the process of communication there are implicit presuppositions that each person holds about the other which affect the nature of the messages transmitted. For good communication, it is important to know how people perceive each other and their own social context.

As an example, a sexist male may talk to a woman he is dating as he "perceives" her in a certain role. This is irritating to the woman who may feel that he is not relating to her as an equal. The situation is compounded if she personalizes this situation and responds assuming he is "putting her down." She can react in two ways:

1. by getting angry and telling him directly that he is sexist, or
2. by telling him how she feels. If she interacts on a "feeling level" she will tell him that she feels "put down" by his attitude toward her. This response is more likely to generate greater understanding between them.

THE COMPLEXITY OF COMMUNICATION SCRIPTS

Many of the assumptions that influence our perception of the environment and characteristics of your employer/family, other nannies, friends, etc. have been internalized through the process of socialization or conditioning. These perceptions are not easily changed. Such internalization are called scripts. These scripts are specific sequences of events that are expected by the individual. For example, a middle-aged adult develops scripts about interacting with his/her co-workers by experience. The child will establish his own script on how to interact with elderly adults by noticing how his parents and others perform in such situations. Another example is the person who always raises their voice when speaking to an elderly person, which implies that they perceive all elderly as hard of hearing. This can be very insulting to an elderly person who hears as well as you or I. Such scripts can facilitate or complicate the process of communication.

Another complicating factor in the process of communication is that of stereotyping. A stereotype is an over-simplified mental image of some category of person. A stereotype is shared in essential features by large numbers of people. Stereotypes are sometimes accompanied by prejudice, i.e. by a favorable or unfavorable predisposition towards any member of the category in question, with little consideration given to the idea that each one of us is an individual.

A common categorization method used by people is identifying those who are "like us" and those who are "not like us." For example, a white person may categorize everyone black as "not like us," and everyone white "like us," or consider all older people as alike and therefore as having little in common with him.

NON-VERBAL COMMUNICATION

Non-verbal communication plays an important role in your communication with your employer/family. Non-verbal cues can have greater influence upon the outcome of a communication than verbal cues. Examples of non-verbal cues include lack of respect, subordination, information anxiety, and self-conceit. All forms of behavior become potential messages when people communicate—action and inaction, interest and indifference—all convey information to the other.

ASSERTION

Assertion is a style of behavior which acknowledges the value of your own needs and convictions in a manner that respects the needs and convictions of others. Assertive behavior functions between the extremes of not being able to share a conviction (non-assertiveness) and forcing a conviction on others (aggressiveness). Assertiveness involves both attitudes and behavior.

- An assertive attitude depends on your appreciation of your own experiences, needs, and purposes. A conviction that your own perceptions and goals are of value is basic to mature assertion. As assertive attitude then involves self-awareness, self-disclosure, and self-worth. These are described as follows:
- Self-awareness: In order to pursue your own needs and purposes, you must be aware of what they are. You must know what you have experienced, what you think, how you feel, what you need, and what you want to do.

- Self-disclosure: Are you able to express your ideas, your needs, your purposes. This requires skill and will. In terms of skill, you must be able to state your position. You must have the words to express yourself appropriately so that you may be understood. This may bring up a question of vocabulary: Do you have the right words to express yourself accurately in a variety of different situations?
- Self worth: What you are and what you have to say is important. Your ideas may not always be right—or best, but they are worthwhile and worth discussing, thinking about and sharing. If you do not feel secure in your own self-worth, it will be difficult to convey your thoughts, ideas, and feelings to others.

Common Obstacles To Healthy Communication

One of the most common obstacles to good communication is the inability or reluctance to deal with issues directly, honestly, and in a timely manner. This should occur before the issue becomes emotionally charged or out of proportion.

Another common obstacle is the tendency of some people to overreact. When issues are blown out of proportion communication is blocked. This occurs when we focus on the negative aspects of an issue, compounding it, rather than dealing with it directly, honestly, and in a timely manner.

Some people can work themselves up into an extremely negative, non-productive state of mind when the issues are exaggerated. It is far better to focus on a solution to an issue, right from the start, rather than to focus on its negative aspects.

A good example of blocked communication is the nanny who feels that her boss doesn't appreciate her. She can easily escalate her anxiety about the situation by telling herself:

a) "I never get the respect I deserve."
b) "It's just not fair that the boss doesn't notice bow much I put into my job."

c)   "I don't deserve this kind of humiliation."

d)   "I can't stand being treated like this another day.", etc.

Directing your communication by concentrating on a solution right away usually requires much less energy. It will help you solve the issue quickly. By doing this you will feel better psychologically since you will be in a positive (rather than negative) productive state of mind. Talking to a friend who can be objective is also helpful.

Developing A Therapeutic Attitude

Once you've developed the ability to concentrate on positive problem solving rather than avoidance or overreacting to problems, your attitude and demeanor toward the children you are caring for and the adults you are working with will be much more therapeutic. Other skills are also helpful in maintaining a therapeutic attitude. Projecting both an empathetic and non-judgmental attitude can help you do this.

Empathy

Empathy can be described as the professional's ability to feel for the person they are caring for and to respond to them in a way that lets them know that the professional is "in-tune" with their feelings. The professional is in a sense validating, acknowledging, and accepting that the person has these feelings and never denying, or minimizing them.

COMMUNICATING WITH PARENTS—DOS AND DON'TS

SET AN AGENDA. Decide on the topic for discussion, pick a place where there are no distraction, and agree on how much time will be allotted, with the understanding that there may be future meeting set up. Keep focused on the current issues and keep track of time.

BE PATIENT. Despite the fact that some people are slow talkers, don't interrupt.

FOCUS ON POSITIVE RESULTS. Hold the belief that everyone's needs can be met in a satisfactory and enjoyable way. There are solutions that can work for everyone. The challenge is to honor everyone involved and be open to all possibilities. It may take several meetings to explore and create the most workable environment.

ALLOW EACH PERSON TO SPEAK WITHOUT INTERRUPTION. Listen to what each person has to say with an open mind. Let go of judging and evaluating. This allows each person to express their feelings freely and comfortably. Often it is helpful to use a "talking stick" or another object to designate the speaker. Person with the object speaks, while the others listen intently, with each receiving the opportunity to respond and express feelings when the speaker is done and the object is passed.

GIVE EMPATHY. Acknowledge each other's feelings and needs. (see chapter on High Self-esteem). Practicing empathy instead of opposition or intellectual feedback can bring remarkable results in creating nurturing, mutually supportive relationships.

TALK HONESTLY ABOUT YOUR FEELINGS AND CONCERNS. Know that you have a right to express your feeling without being accusing, or making anyone else wrong. Take a few moments so that you can state them clearly and directly without being overly emotional.

DEVELOP AN INQUIRING ATTITUDE. Ask open ended questions. For example: "What was that like?"

USE "I STATEMENTS." Avoid defensive reactions by coming from your own personal experience. Instead of beginning with accusations that begin with "you," shift the tone by stating how you feel. For example: "When I heard what you did, I felt really angry because I felt like my input was being ignored."

PARAPHRASE. Done correctly, this avoids enormous assumptions.

USE EXPANDERS ("TELL ME MORE"). This conveys interest and inquiry. Use eye contact and nodding of the head.

BEGIN AND END WITH SOMETHING POSITIVE. Acknowledge the positive aspects or qualities of the situation or individuals involved before addressing frustrating or difficult issues, End on a positive note by thanking others for their time and effort in participating in the communication process. This approach keeps problems in perspective and avoids the perception that everything is going wrong.

As the Nanny learns to listen to herself and others through effective communication, she develops a keen sense of her own strengths and weaknesses. Improved self-esteem for all concerned is an inevitable by-product. By mindfully tuning into the communication process, the Nanny becomes adept at recognizing her own feelings as well as the emotional states of others. She learns self-monitoring techniques and skills in linking causes and emotions. Learning consideration of another's view point, leads to greater tolerance of others and the realization of how one's behavior can effect other people.

When the inevitable conflict arises, it is often met by avoidance or resistance. This only leads to discomfort and magnification of the problem. Instead of denying conflict, embracing and understanding it can become one of the greatest gifts for positive growth and change.

Steps for Interpersonal Problem Solving

1. Stop and think, identify the problems and feelings about them.
2. Decide on a goal, generate alternative solutions, evaluate their possible consequences, select the best and plan to execute it.
3. Try the formulated plan.
4. Evaluate the outcome, try another solution and/or plan, or alternatively reevaluate the goal if an obstacle results in failure to reach the intended goal.

THE NON-JUDGMENTAL ATTITUDE

The ability to be non-judgmental is another necessary factor in maintaining an open line of communication. If the empathetic professional acknowledges and "accepts" the feelings and emotions of the other person, they must also be non-judgmental or objective in the way that they respond to them. Being non-judgmental means that we refrain from forming a personal opinion on the actions or feelings of our employers. This is especially important in instances when our opinion of how a situation should be bandied is different than the parents', i.e. responding to a 5 year olds bullying treatment of a younger child.

Being non-judgmental means that we don't "glorify" ourselves in the communication process by telling the person about how we "handled a similar situation" and "did this or that." This implies that our opinions or assessment of the situation are best, thus passing judgment on the person eventual action or lack of action.

Allowing others to exercise their free choice about how a particular situation should be handled—especially parents (and children, whenever appropriate) is one of the hallmarks of the true Nanny. It is, in fact, a demonstration of respect toward another when we accept their views, opinions, etc. Non-judgmentally, acknowledging that it is the other person's right to have and exorcise their own opinion.

GUIDELINES FOR COMMUNICATING WITH CHILDREN

- Be observant of your own moods and affect and make the effort to maintain a positive attitude even on difficult days. (This is one of the major differences between a skilled Nanny and a baby sitter.)
- Observe how the parents interact with each child:
  a) which methods are effective?
  b) which aren't?

- Copy whatever methods the parents employ which are effective.
- Avoid baby talk or improper terminologies, i.e. your pee pee instead of your penis, deliberately mispronouncing words.
- Be simple when communicating with children, avoid lengthy explanations unless an older child needs more inform

- Use diversionary techniques, a limit setting tool.
- Exert enthusiasm when reading to or playing with children, or when using diversionary techniques.
- Talk to them respectfully, as you would any other individual.
- Never name call, i.e. bad boy/girl—this is damaging to a child's self-esteem and teaches that name calling is acceptable behavior.
- Never engage in power struggles or arguments if a child does not want to do what you want. Do one of the following:

  a) Drop the matter if it is unimportant
  b) Clearly state the consequences if the child does not do as you tell her, i.e., "You'll have to leave the room if you throw that block again," and follow through.
  c) Divert the child's attention to something else.

- Remember that a child as young as six months will start to comprehend some of what you say. The older the child, the more he understands. Avoid talking about the child as though he either doesn't understand or is not present. Never talk about children's parents in front of them or discuss adult matters which may confuse or upset them.
- When appropriate, tell the child how you feel as it relates to your interaction with him, i.e., "I feel angry when you write on the wall," "I'm tired and I'm not very patient." This teaches children to recognize feelings and talk about them, rather than name calling or using other socially unacceptable behaviors.
- Never use guilt tactics, i.e., "Wait until Mom hears what you did. She'll be so sad."
- Listen with your full attention when a child is talking to you, be aware of your body language and facial expressions. These non-verbal cues will convey interest or lack of interest.

- If you can't give a child your attention say so, along with telling him when he'll have your attention, i.e., "Just a minute. As soon as I finish talking with Mrs. Smith, I'll be with you."
- Talk about feelings, i.e., "You look sad, Joey. Is something wrong?" or "I'm sorry if your angry at me, Joey, but it's too late to play outside."
- Do not give unrealistic choices, i.e., Nanny to two year old, "Do you want to take your nap now?" Instead say, "It's time for your nap, which story would you like today?" (with enthusiasm).

WRITTEN COMMUNICATION—NANNY'S DAILY LOG

Upon the parent's return, the Nanny will always inform the parents how the children ate, slept, etc. After an evening out, sitters who are merely adequate often don't think of this and sometimes the parents are either too busy or too tired to ask. For the following reasons, the Nanny ALWAYS keeps parents informed using the daily log.

Important information will be maintained since it is written.

- Habits, behaviors, etc. will be recognized because a written sequence of events is available, i.e. poor eating habits, etc.
- Parents will have a clearer perception of how their children spend their time, providing an opportunity to evaluate the quality of time spent.
- Parents will feel more knowledgeable and involved with their children since this detailed information is available.
- Without the Daily Log, important milestones, trends, etc. in development may be missed or forgotten.
- The Daily Log format reinforces what areas the Nanny must be observant of.

This can be accomplished using an inexpensive notebook and is kept "diary-style" with entries made daily. It should be left in a common area such as the kitchen or study, where both the Nanny and parents can have easy access to it.

The "Standard Nanny-Family Agreement" addresses continuity of care. Continuity of care is represented in part by this method of passing information. The term "Continuity of Care" means that the care children receive from both the Nanny and Parent is consistent, which can only occur if information is passed on.

Example

As an example, lack of continuity of care is described in the following situations:

Situation 1: The child you are caring for does not have an appetite on a particular day and is cranky and uncooperative. She also refuses to take her nap. When the parents come home from work, you leave immediately, after telling them some information about your day, only mentioning crankiness. (Any one of these things alone is not a big issue, but together have definite implications for how the evening may go!)

Situation 2: The child does not have an appetite for dinner, continues to be cranky and appears fatigued. Since the parents have not been informed that the child missed lunch, they now being to suspect that perhaps the child ate a big lunch or perhaps had a late snack. Because she does not want dinner, they are not sure if they should be concerned or not. Since the child is cranky, they wonder how long a nap the child bad or what time the child got up from her nap. Not realizing that the child not only did not sleep, but also did not eat much all day, the parents wonder what is wrong with the child.

Situation 3: They are all tired and do not have much patience dealing with the child. The parents are left wondering "Did she have a good nap?" "Did she have a late snack and/or a big lunch?" "Is this crankiness a 'stage' she's beginning to go through?" etc.

The amount of quality time working (or otherwise occupied) parents spend with their children is vital to healthy family relationships. The Nanny will be certain to pass on important (and sometimes what may seem to be redundant and unimportant) information via the Daily Log each and every day.

Keeping the Daily Log:

The components of the log are based in part on basic human needs. Some of the basic needs to include in your daily log are: activity/exercise, appetite/diet, elimination, and growth/development. When commenting on these areas, do so in a narrative style, rather than writing "ate tuna salad and apple for lunch," make comments on appetite, compare to bow well the child eats at other meals, etc.

Make it as interesting as possible for providing related information. Remark on the child's (or children's) activity level. This will include comments such as…

"did not participate in playgroup as usual"

"appeared tired,"

"seems to be getting bored with toys"

"can easily do all puzzles"

"purchase more advanced puzzles?"

"has started to climb, (elaborate)

"suggest we check security of bookcase in room to be sure it cannot fall over," etc. "is taking a longer afternoon nap and not as long a morning nap."

"is resisting unstructured playtime, does not seem interested in independent play—will have to come up with some ideas for making unstructured time more interesting."

"Woke up several times last night."

"Nightmares—we should discuss how to handle this." "Has refused lunch again today—how well is he eating at dinner?"

"Shall we try different foods?"

"Asking for a bottle 3-4 times each day—should we discuss this?"

(Note: When to begin potty training should be the parents' decision.)

"Refused to Sit on potty"

"Used the potty, had a small bowel movement"

"Has not moved bowels for 2 days, shall we increase bulk in diet?"

"Have given her fruit twice today."

An Outline for Nanny's Daily Log

On the following page you will find an outline that you can use as a guide for your own Daily Log. This is the place to note the occurrence of new skills observed, i.e., motor, language, etc. To differentiate between children, use initials.

Nanny's Daily Log

Parent &Nanny Notes: Today's Date_____

_____
_____
_____
_____
_____

PHYSICAL EXERCISE:
i.e.. playground. played ball. Walks, any physical activity, "cruising, climbing, etc.

_____
_____

REST/SLEEP
Awake at: _____ am.
Napped from:_____ to_____
Quiet time from: _____ to_____
Asleep at:_____ p.m.

DIET/NUTRITION: List what was eaten at what times After each entry, please specify if the child ate well, fair or poorly; include any liquids consumed throughout the day:

~Multivitamins taken or any other supplement_____ ~Medications (See EZ-Dose-It form)

~Breakfast, _____

~ Lunch, _____

~Snacks _____

~Dinner, _____

ELIMINATION:

~Diaper changes times: (note any rash) _____

~Bowel movements (time: note normal, loose etc, note any rash)_____

_____

~Potty Training Notes_____

_____

HYGIENE:
Make a check after each item as it is accomplished

~Washed hands after using bathroom:_____
~Brushed teeth after each meal: _____
~Gums wiped before bedtime (infants without teeth only) _____
~Fingernails checked:. Cleaned: _____ Trimmed: _____
~Toenails checked: Cleaned: _____ Trimmed: _____
~Hair Brushed/Styled: _____
~Bathed: _____ Hair Washed: _____
~Clothing Clean: _____ Fits Properly: _____ Wrinkle Free: _____

GROWTH & DEVELOPMENT MILESTONES:
Your comments and observations regarding each child's Physical, Cognitive, Social & Psychological growth & development should be included each day.

1. Physical = anything that has to do with physical activity
(Took a first step, made it to the top of the jungle gym, rolled over, measured; grew two inches since___ An infant's ability to hold her head up, beginning to crawl, walk, climb) Coordination, i.e. riding a tricycle, two-wheeler, etc

_____

2. Cognitive = anything that has to do with intellect, learning, speaking
(New skills, saying new words, examples of how an infant has shown she understands something that was said. Counting, ABC's, recognition)

3. Social = anything that has to do with interacting with other children or adults
(Your observations of child's reaction to new people, interacting with an age-mate, reaction to strangers, sharing, hitting, a pre-verbal child attempting to communicate, etc.)

4. Psychological = anything that has to do with moods, feelings, emotions
(Talking about feelings: friends, school, pets, neighbors, etc. Note any crying and your observations about why, anger, jealousy, humor, anxiety, frustration, etc. Emergence of new personality traits, moods, fears, attachment to specific toys, people, blanket, bottle. Reoccurrence (regression) thumb-sucking, bedwetting, etc.)

Hours worked today; _____–_____   Nanny's initials_____

PROCESS RECORDING

The Process Recording is a learning tool. If practiced, it will result in more effective communicating skills. The purpose of the Process Recording is to learn to overcome the normal inhibitions many people experience when they are faced with the prospect of expressing their needs, rights, or ideas. It is important in any relationship to be able to express your true feelings directly and to be able to let the appropriate person know when your feelings or rights have been overlooked. The overall objective of practicing Process Recordings is to become comfortable discussing issues directly, honestly in a non-threatening manner and before they become out-of-proportion. One Process Recording each week should be done until nine out often Process Recordings are productive and a healthy line of communication is established.

GUIDELINES:

The Process Recording is an organized Planned Communication Exercise. The steps are:

1. Determine subject to be discussed.
2. Identify purpose and objectives.
3. Define your points of emphasis. These are statement/questions relating to feelings or facts.
4. During the exercise write down the other person's points of emphasis.
5. Review both points of emphasis (yours and other individuals).
6. Evaluate productivity of the exchange.

The following is an example of a Process Recording on "Privacy." Other subjects are:

- Salary increase (when, criteria, how much)
- Termination of your commitment period (will you extend, train someone else, etc.)
- Use of vehicle (who pays for gas, limits, etc.)
- Overnight guests (friends vs. family, etc.)

Nanny's needs for time away from the family and or home (i.e. to be with friends or to pursue personal interests).

To provide an opportunity for both the Nanny and the employer to openly talk about their respective need for privacy. This is a means of establishing a healthy line of communication.

1. Make a list of "points of emphasis" (areas/topics you want to discuss). Do this before you begin.
    ~I would like to be able to have friends sleep over from time to time.
    ~As a responsible person, I do not expect to have a curfew, but expect that you understand that my time off is "my own time." However, I do understand that I am a role model for your children and I do not intend to conduct myself in an undignified way at any time. How will my coming and going be disruptive to you on my time off?
    ~I would like to know if there are times when you, as a family, would like to spend time alone, so that I can make other plans."
    ~There are times when I need to be alone in my room, and those times are...
    ~There are times when I like to sleep late on the weekend.

2.) Make a list of the "points of emphasis" that the family brought up, in addition to listing YOUR "points of emphasis."
3.) In conclusion, tell how productive or non-productive the meeting was.

CHAPTER FIVE

Ethics for Child Care Professionals

THE ETHICAL DYNAMIC

What makes an act "ethical?" For most people, society, to a large extent, dictates their ideas about what is right and wrong. Religion and spirituality also play major roles in how a person may view a particular act, as being ethical, or unethical. However, in order for a person to be able to make ethical decisions, there are some vital personality characteristics, which they must possess, in order to be able to make a well thought out ethical decision.

PERSONAL VALUES

Our parents and family situation largely shape personal values. Many times, however, what we learned at home and what the world is showing us may conflict. The early twenties is the time period during which we reconcile these conflicting beliefs. This is also the time period during which Nannys are beginning their career. It is not unusual for many of us to have conflicting feeling about important issues such as: capital punishment, abortion, gay tights, parent's who use corporal punishment, just to name a few. What is essential, however, is your willingness to take the time to explore your feelings about any issue that impacts on you, either personally, or as a professional. Therefore, the important thing is to pause and consider the possibility that you may not have clarity around your own personal beliefs, on a given topic. That's why the Ethical Dynamic is an important process. Another important consideration should you be helping another person, a friend or an adolescent sort out her ethical dilemma is; what are HER personal values in this situation, and how can you help her gain clarity for herself, as opposed to imposing your values on her?

INTELLECT

To be able to engage in what we refer to as the "Ethical Dynamic," one must possess the intellectual capacity to think through the various alternatives she/he may take in pursuing the best action. One must be able to think abstractly in terms of looking at the various options which she/be is faced with in dealing with the problems at hand, and then follow each option in her mind to its probable conclusion. Once this is done with every single probable outcome of each option, only then can she determine which option is the most ethical choice to pursue. The person faced with making the ethical decision then realizes that there may not be an easy answer. Many times what is required is the ability and good judgment to choose the course of action which may create temporary anxiety and tension, and perhaps anger, on the part of others, because it is simply the right thing to do.

SELF-AWARENESS

Being involved in the ethical decision-making process is an anxiety-provoking experience for most people. However, it is vital to maintain the self-awareness to know why you may be leaning in one direction versus the other in terms of which action you will take to resolve the problem in the best possible way. As stated earlier in the text, society dictates it's good, and it's bad values to us. "Don't get involved" is one of our society's values' which encourages the cynic in each of us to look the other way when we see that someone is being harmed, has been harmed, or probably will be harmed. As Nannys, we are "Mandated Reporters," meaning that we are lawfully required to report any *suspicions* we may have about a child being harmed in any way. The Key word here is "Suspicions". It is not necessary for a Mandated Reporter to have proof. It is not your responsibility to prove anything. Rather your responsibility is to protect any child whom you suspect may be being abused by reporting it.

As long as people refuse to get "involved," child abuse, domestic abuse, emotional abuse, and other crimes will continue to proliferate. We each have a responsibility to get involved. On the opposite side of the "don't get involved" cynicism, is the "control-freak." The controlling person may derive a sense of power in the ethical dynamic as he/she thinks through the various possible outcomes of each option, and recognizes the impact his/her decision may have. The desire to "Handle it myself" may indicate that the person doing the handling may have some control issues which are likely interfering with making the best ethical decision.

COURAGE

A vital ingredient in the Ethical Dynamic is the courage to follow through and do the right thing. As we go through the steps intellectually we imagine how others may react and how they may perceive us. We know there is someone, in every situation that is a strong believer in: "Don't get involved." In fact, some people are so committed to this philosophy that they believe that anyone who does get involved is making a foolish choice.

We know that there is always the possibility that our actions and our best intentions will backfire, leaving us feeling confused about whether or not we did the right thing. And this is where the courage comes in.

The most important thing is that we take the necessary steps to resolve whatever the problem is AND to be able to let go of attachment to the end result. In other words, each of us needs to stand up for we believe in, speak out about things which we believe are not right, especially when someone is being harmed, has been harmed, or could possibly be harmed, and then let the situation be handled by others, whenever appropriate.

It cannot be emphasized enough, how important it is to always, always, seek out the opinion of an objective third party to help in the decision-making process, regardless of the strength of your own self-awareness, or personal convictions about what is right or wrong Hotlines exist and are listed in the front, or back of every telephone book. Social services, such as Children's Protective Service, are staffed with people who are the best resources to utilize. Any of these resources can be used anonymously. Use these hotlines to assist in the process, even when you are sure of what to do.

Maintaining Confidentiality

Working in your employer's private home means that you will be privy to more information about their; habits, lifestyle, martial or family issues, etc. than you would care to know. The saying "I don't need to know that" was probably first spoken by a nanny!

It is absolutely essential that we respect the confidences of others. In Nanny-Family relationships, however, you are held to an even higher standard, because you are working professionally. Just as a doctor, lawyer, or priest cannot discuss or divulge confidential information that they learned during the course of fulfilling their duties, nannies also are held to that same code of ethics. Trust is a vital ingredient of the Nanny-Family relationship.

Teaching values & helping children understand the concept of Ethical behavior

- Seek out age-appropriate books dealing with values for the children you care for. Your librarian is a great resource for this.
- Read aloud to your children, regardless of their age, even older kids enjoy hearing a story. *Chicken Soup For The Soul* is a great compilation of short stories which can be read to babies, as well as pre-teens (it's good for you too, it will restore your faith in the goodness of the human race!).
- If you use videos to entertain your children, choose those with a "moral" to the story, these are available for all ages. Talk about it after watching it together.
- Avoid cartoons, soap opera's, violent "action films, or anything that is giving the viewer a negative message. The subliminal impact of these materials is very strong.
- *Teaching your Child Values* by Linda and Richard Eyre
- Volunteer at a soup kitchen or shelter; take your child(ren) so everyone can get involved.
- Practice "random acts of kindness"—the best way to teach is by example.

Other considerations

Children learn by example and we are their earliest teachers. We all know that small children look up to the adults in their lives and some believe that their parents, or nanny can do no wrong. In other words, whatever the special adults in their lives do—*must* be right. As far as the child is concerned what they see and hear the adults do or say is *the* way to do it.

Think about the following ad what you are (teaching) your child;

~Your charge sometimes hears you say when the telephone rings; "Tell him I'm not here right now", (how to lie)

~Your three year old charge takes a pack of gum off the shelf in the check-out line at the grocery store after everything has been rung up. You ignore it, after all, you both shared half of the bag of grapes before you got to the register, (stealing is okay)

~Your five year old overhears you talking unfavorably on the telephone about her mother (your employer). Soon after that, mom arrives home. Your demeanor when your boss arrives is completely different than your tone when talking about her on the telephone just before her arrival, (how to be superficial)

~You are with your child at a playgroup where nannies are discussing their salaries. A child overhears his nanny talk about his parents saying: "You should see the way they spend money, you would think they'd get their priorities straight and pay me what I deserve to take care of their child" (how to be critical and judgmental)

~Nanny to nine year old; "Don't tell mommy we went to MacDonald's for dinner and I won't say anything about what your teacher told me, ok? We'll just keep it between us" (It's okay to lie)

~A nanny tells her child: "You told your sister not to tell me you went over to Tommy's house after school, didn't you?" "I'm very disappointed in you for not being honest" (it's okay for adults to lie, but not children)

Shielding Children from Inappropriate Issues;

One of the Nanny's duties is to preserve and protect her child's psychological well-being. Too often, adults speak either in front of children, is a close enough proximity so that the child can overhear the conversation. It is very destructive for a child to hear negative or unkind things, or even information they don't understand about their parents or anyone who is important to them—including their nanny.

Bear in mind that children may understand conversation as early as five or six months of age. Children notice different tones of voices, inflections, sarcasm, anger, etc. even if they cannot understand the meaning of the words. They recognize their parents names and names of others who are important in their lives, when heard.

It is critical that we understand that it can create anxiety, tension and insecurity for children to overhear or be subjected to information that it is inappropriate for them. Too often we forget about this, especially with preverbal children. No one would intentionally subject a child to what we commonly believe to be inappropriate, such as scary stories, gruesome news reports, etc. It is as important to shield children from hearing about negative matters or issues, especially about people they love. Proper ethical conduct includes refraining from any activities, situations or conversations that could create anxiety, stress or worry on the part of a child.

We all have both positive and negative feelings about people that we work for, live with, care about or even those who are just acquaintances. It is not wrong to have opinions, or conflicted feelings. It is however, wrong to discuss these matters if there is *any* possibility that a child made overhear the conversation. This cannot be emphasized enough. A good rule of thumb is to keep conversations that would be inappropriate for child to overhear, completely out of the workplace.

PART TWO

Child Development Skills

CHAPTER SIX

Keeping Children Safe

Curiosity is the driving force behind education, and fortunately, children are born with an overwhelming abundance of it. During the first six months of life, their visual and auditory skills become sharpened and they gradually gain greater control over the different parts of their bodies. They soak up everything they can with their eyes and ears, and whatever they can reach they actively explore with their hands, fingers and mouths. As they enter the second half of the first year, they are very much aware of everything in the world around them, but they do not as yet have the capacity to get too much of it on their own.

Children usually learn to crawl when they are between six and nine months of age. Soon after that they begin pulling themselves up to stand and learning to walk ("cruising"—walking while holding onto something). Eventually they start to walk—and climb. Now they not only have the intense desire to get into and around everything, but they also have the ability to do so. Children at this stage of life would rather explore their world than do almost anything else.

When children begin to explore their world, they accomplish an amazing amount of learning. We adults have been around houses and yards for quite a while and have become a bit jaded, so we forget how interesting and exciting just about everything is when it is being seen, heard, smelled, tasted, touched, pushed, pulled, dropped or whatever for the first time. In the opinion of many experts, the potential for learning from these experiences makes 6–36 months the most important educational period in the lives of young children.

Unfortunately, it also is the most dangerous period. It takes quite awhile for children's knowledge to catch up with their curiosity. While they are interested in and excited by everything, infants and toddlers are also totally naive about everything. As a result, hospital emergency wards report that accidental falls, poisonings and other serious mishaps are more common during this period than at any other time of life. Furthermore, Nannies and parents routinely report that during this period, the life expectancy of plants, glassware, appliances, treasured family heirlooms, etc. could be at an all-time low.

As the child's Nanny, you can choose one of two strategies for dealing with this situation. The first involves restricting the child to a small but safe area, such as a single room or a playpen, except for a few moments each day when the child can be carefully supervised. While the child is restricted, you can provide lots of "educational" toys. When you are with the child, you can provide a host of "educational" games and activities.

The second strategy involves childproofing the home and keeping it childproof for two or three years. Anything that can cause damage to the child—as well as anything the child can damage—can be removed, locked up or otherwise disposed of. With the home thus made safe for and from the child, the child can then be allowed to roam about and explore pretty much alone and at will all day long.

Both strategies are loving, well meant and dedicated to the child's best interests. However, if you choose the first strategy, the child will be largely uninspired and unfulfilled. As the months go by curiosity will wane and, for the most part, educational development will slow down considerably. Conversely, if you choose the second strategy, the child's curiosity will continue to expand and educational development will advance in leaps and bounds. As long as the child is well supervised, the little adventurer will be much better off than when restricted.

Consequently, making the home safe for and from newly crawling children should be one of the Nanny's top priorities. Since children develop at different rates and seem to revel in pulling off surprises, it is suggested that some of these "surprises" be anticipated. Childproofing of the home should be started when they are only four or five months of age. It may involve a fair amount of inconvenience and effort, but the importance for promoting children's educational development and general well-being cannot be stressed enough, not to mention the contribution such education will make to maintaining the sanity of the Nanny.

Here are a few helpful hints for changing a home from a danger zone into a learning environment:

THE KITCHEN

Infants and toddlers spend more time in the kitchen than any other room in the house. The reason is that Nannies tend to spend a lot of time there during the children's waking hours, and children generally prefer to be near their Nanny—even if they are more interested in explorations than social interactions. Therefore, this is the first and foremost place to make safe.

The Stove—The typical kitchen is filled with a variety of wonderful things for the child to investigate. It also contains a variety of serious hazards. Some things simply cannot be made safe and should be ruled out-of-bounds at all times. The stove is a good example. Even when you're not using it, the child may decide to see what happens when those funny knobs are turned. When you are using it, make sure the child does not learn the lesson about touching hot stoves the hard and painful way. If you are boiling or frying on top of the stoves use back burners to avoid splatter problems. If any pots or pans are on the front burners, turn handles inward so the child cannot reach up and grab them.

Storage Bins, Cupboards, Shelves, And Drawers—Your first task is to take an inventory of everything that is potentially dangerous in the hands of the child. Cleansers, polishes, detergents, insecticides, and various other liquids and powders can be lethal. If they are not really needed, get rid of them. If they are, store them in a drawer or a cabinet that can be locked. Sharp utensils such as knives, forks, graters, etc., should likewise be locked away.

Pots And Pans—The remaining items can provide the child with hours of fun and learning, and you can help by making them more accessible. For your own sake, you may want to keep the flour out of reach, but for the child's sake, fill up the low cupboards and shelves with pots and pans, plastic cups and bowls, spoons and spatulas, canned goods and paper products, etc. Just keep the heavier items on the lowest levels so as to prevent harmful avalanches.

Appliances—Make sure that the garbage pail has a lid that the child cannot remove, and keep all plastic bags and wrappings out of reach. Unplug, and if possible, remove coffee makers, toasters, irons and other appliances when not in use. When they are in use, see to it that the electrical cords are not dangling over the edge of the counter where the child can grab and pull them. Be mindful of doors on refrigerators, dishwashers, washers and dryers, and other such items that are attractive but inappropriate choices for a game of "hide and seek."

Things to Do to Keep the Kitchen Safe

- Make an inventory of everything in drawers, bins, cabinets and shelves and evaluate for safety.
- Use back burners on stove instead of front, whenever possible.
- Turn handles of pans inward on stove.
- Remove or prevent a swinging door from moving.
- Make the stove, counter tops and tabletop absolutely off limits.
- Let the child have his or her own drawer or an area of the kitchen where toys can be kept.

- Unplug appliances when not in use.
- Be mindful not to leave utensils within reach while in use, should you put them down for a moment
- Be aware of and prevent the possibility of a child climbing into an opening that can close behind him, e.g., a dryer door.
- Buckets of water are responsible for many deaths each year. Empty all buckets immediately.

Things to Keep Out of Reach in the Kitchen

- Knives, forks, peelers, graters—anything sharp
- Plastic wrap and the box with jagged edges in which it is packaged.
- Detergents, e.g., dishwasher, soap, cleansers, polishes, insecticides, etc.
- Dangling cords, e.g., telephone, appliances, window blinds, etc.

THE BATHROOM

The typical bathroom contains an amazing amount of potentially exciting experiences for the child. The child will love to frolic in the bathtub and play at the sink, and there are few activities that can rival an opportunity to flush the toilet when it comes to fun and fascination. Unfortunately, because of all the slippery surfaces, sharp objects and toxic substances, it is virtually impossible to make a bathroom completely safe, so it should be off-limits unless supervision is available.

Even though you make it off-limits, make sure that razors, scissors, clippers, etc. are kept in locked drawers, and that soaps, shampoos, creams, etc. are likewise securely stored when not in use. Be especially vigilant with pills and potions. The medicine cabinet should be kept locked at all times and old remedies should be disposed of carefully and quickly as soon as they are no longer needed. When the child is at the sink or in the tub, appliances such as electric razors, curling irons and radios should be well beyond reach.

Things to Do to Keep the Bathroom Safe

- Water heater temperature control should be adjusted to 120° Fahrenheit or less to prevent scalds.
- Make it off limits for exploration.
- Secure laundry chute.
- Never allow rough housing while bathing.
- Faucet guards to prevent child from turning water on.
- Unplug all appliances.
- Door locks too high to reach so child cannot lock him/herself in.
- Dispose of expired medications or any that are not needed.
- Install non-scalding device (plumber usually installs).

Things to Keep Out of Reach in the Bathroom

- Razors, scissors, clippers in locked drawers.
- Soaps, shampoos, creams out of reach.
- Medicines locked up.
- Keep all small appliances, e.g., curling irons, in a secure place away from water.

THE BEDROOM

The typical bedroom seems to be made for babies. The bed is soft and there are plenty of puffy pillows with which to play. The floor is usually carpeted and most of the furniture is either simple and low, or large and stable. Moreover, the drawers and closets contain a multitude of materials to be searched and studied. You will be amazed at the enjoyment the child will get out of everything from a pair of old slippers to a pile of freshly folded laundry. However, there are a few subtle hazards of which to be wary: Cosmetics, perfumes, deodorants, shoe polish and other such things can be poisonous. Jewelry, beads, buttons, etc. are items can cause choking if swallowed. Make sure these items are stored securely out of reach. Do not put too much faith in high places, such as the chest-of-drawers. (A two-year-old can very cleverly pull out the bottom drawer, step on it so he or she can step on the next drawer, step on it, and so on until she has managed to reach the top.)

ODDS AND ENDS

- ➢ A full-length mirror on the wall or door will be endlessly fascinating for the child, but make sure it is fastened securely and won't fall off.
- ➢ If there are radiators, or if space heaters or fans are used, see to it that they are covered or in some other way protected from prying fingers.
- ➢ If there is a trunk, cedar chest, or similar storage device, fix it so that the heavy lid will not close unexpectedly, thereby catching hands and arms, or even trapping the child inside.

THE LIVING ROOM

There is no such thing as the "typical" living room. Perhaps no other place in the house reflects each family's particular preferences in procuring and positioning their possessions. Most contain an ample supply of chairs to climb on, areas to explore and items to investigate—but it is extremely important that you check out everything from the child's perspective before turning him or her loose. Things that are comfortable and attractive from an adult's point of view may be considerably less so when they are looked at through the eyes of a child.

A Case Study

A couple had designed a living room that was perfectly arranged for their favorite activities and perfectly suited to their tastes. Unfortunately, it also was extremely hazardous to their child's health—a complete catalog of inappropriate and dangerous items and situations.

The focal point of the room was a large fireplace. They had a screen in front of it, but it was made of glass. While it kept the baby from crawling into the fire, the baby could get badly burned just touching the hot surface. Next to the fireplace on either side were attractive piles of round logs that could come tumbling down if the child tried climbing up on them. In front of the fireplace were two beautiful antique rocking chairs, which provided comfortable seating for the couple, but also an excellent opportunity for the child's fingers to get crushed.

In order to read while sitting in the room, the couple had placed lovely porcelain lamps on small tables next to each rocker with extension cords running several feet to the wall outlets. This provided an opportunity for the child to pull the lamps down with a resounding, dangerous and rather expensive crash. The extension cords were frayed, which the couple hardly noticed, but the baby found irresistible. The tables were miniature cast-iron replicas of pot-bellied stoves that would be very harmful if the toddling explorer fell and hit them with her head.

The room had a highly polished hardwood floor with scatter rugs thrown here and there—not much of a problem for the couple but very difficult and dangerous terrain for a new walker to navigate. There was a veritable jungle of exotic plants that made spectacular decorations; however, the temptation was overwhelming for the youngster to pull the vines and pick the leaves, eating whatever would go into her mouth. The coffee table and bookshelves were loaded with various interesting and expensive knickknacks including cigarette lighters and glass vases; and the stereo and videocassette recorder with all their complicated cords, buttons and knobs were on shelves no more than three feet off the floor. It is doubtful these things would remain in place and intact for very long.

It took several hours to redesign this one room. A lot of furniture and fixtures were removed, replaced or refinished with protective tape and bumpers. When it was finished, the room no longer looked like a feature in *Better Homes and Gardens* magazine, but from a safety standpoint the child in this household had fewer accidents, the parents had less aggravation, and in the long run, it was a more relaxing environment.

Thing to Do to Keep a Room Safe

- Make an inventory of what is in each room and evaluate its hazard potential.
- Always wipe up any spilled liquid on floor before a fall occurs.
- Assess bookcases for sturdiness (attach to wall if necessary) and for climbing ease; falls can result.
- Assess furniture with tops that close, e.g., trunks, pianos, toy boxes for lids that could injure fingers, etc.
- Assess furniture for the possibility of a child climbing into them and suffocating, e.g., cedar trunk (chest).
- Assess sturdiness of furniture or fixtures that could easily be pulled over such as lamps and appliances including fans and heaters.
- Place objects in front of radiators, floor furnaces, etc.
- Windows/balconies—keep furniture away from and make safe.

Thing to Keep Out of Reach in Any (Every) Room

- Plants of any kind—know which ones are poisonous.
- Small objects that could be swallowed, e.g., hard candy, cigarette butts.
- Cords, lamps, extensions.
- Fireplace utensils, matches—fireplaces should be blocked.
- Stereo equipment/TV/VCR—keep out of reach on non-climbable objects that lock, if possible.
- Alcohol—lock all liquor cabinets securely.
- Dangling tablecloths.
- Ropes or cords of any kind (avoid toys with cords).

Many Nannies and parents are concerned that if they go out of their way to make the home safe for the newly crawling child, there will be no opportunities to teach the baby the word "no." They feel they should redesign a good portion of the house, but they also feel they should make a special effort to leave a few "don't touch" items out so the child will learn about danger and will learn to respect the notion that he or she cannot have everything wanted.

The sentiments behind such thoughts are good, but you would be mistaken if you put them into practice. First, no matter how good a job childproofing you do, the child will always find things you missed, such as an open safety pin in a shag rug, the fringe of a floor length drape or the broken handle of a tool chest. Anyone who has had to cope with crawling children has experienced this. They will tell you that you will have plenty of chances to say "no," and you certainly don't need to set yourself up for additional aggravation and unnecessary accidents.

Furthermore, while teaching the concept of "no" is important and inevitable, you really don't want to overdo it. The more the child hears your "no" in the course of explorations and investigations, the more the child will begin to associate these activities with the disapproval of someone who means a lot. Moreover, if used too much, "no" begins to lose its effectiveness. An occasional prohibition is far more likely to be heeded than constant restraint. Therefore, do all you can to keep it to a minimum.

Thing to Purchase to Make the Home Safer

- Outlet Covers prevent child from sticking objects into wall outlets, e.g., paper clips, etc.
- Corner Guards—especially important for coffee tables, which are known for their danger to small children (particularly glass top tables).
- Nonskid Strips to attach to scatter rugs to prevent falls as well as for inside tubs and shower stalls
- Cabinet Locks (Latches)—to attach to inside of kitchen, bathroom and living room cabinets
- Lead Paint Detector Kits can be purchased at some drugstores or may be available through your local Board of Health.

Note: You can order "The Perfectly Safe" catalog devoted exclusively to making the home safer for children by calling 1-800-837-KIDS.

Other Considerations

➢ Reevaluate the home regularly (at least monthly) for hazards that may have presented themselves since the home was initially childproofed.

➢ In homes with crawling babies, get down on all fours and look up at the underside of tables, chairs, etc. You may find some hazards that you did not see from a standing position.

GENERAL POLICIES FOR MAINTAINING SAFETY

Automobile

- Always lock doors.
- Never hold a child in your lap in a vehicle.
- Never strap the child in your lap.
- Always use an approved car seat.
- Never use "baby seats" that are not designed specifically for use as car seats.
- Be sure that the seat is used correctly, straps fit snugly (not tight) and seat is securely fastened.
- Never allow children to unbuckle themselves in the car or to become disorderly—pull over and stop the car, if necessary.
- Never allow children to play in a driveway.
- Never leave a child alone in a car, EVER, for any reason.
- Sharp or heavy objects should be kept in the trunk. They can become deadly projectiles in a sudden stop or accident. This is another reason why ALL adult passengers should wear a seat belt, besides the fact it is mandated by law.
- Animals should be restrained.

Burns

- Keep matches and lighters out of reach.
- Always test temperature of foods and liquids before feeding baby, especially when using a microwave that heats unevenly resulting in hot and cold spots in food and liquids.
- Keep appliances out of grasp.
- Block radiators, heaters and fireplaces.
- When bathing, shut off water and keep child away from faucets.
- Keep children out of direct sun in hot weather, and use sun block with a minimum of 15 SPF when outside.

Bathing

- Always check water temperature.
- Use non-skid mats in bathtub and shower.
- Never leave a child in the bathtub or shower without supervision, even for a few seconds. Drowning can occur very quickly.
- Never allow roughhousing in the bathroom; porcelain tubs, toilet bowls and ceramic floors are very hard.

Choking, Smothering

- Know the Heimlich maneuver.
- Assess toys for removable parts that could be chewed or sucked off.
- Never give infants or toddlers items such as nuts, popcorn, hard candy or gum.
- Never allow baby to suck on anything that could break apart and be swallowed, e.g., lollipops, balloons or small objects.
- Never allow infants or toddlers to play with rope or cords. Avoid toys that have ropes attached.
- Never allow or put a necklace on an infant or toddler, e.g., to hold a pacifier.

- Never allow children to play with plastic bags.
- Keep soft pillows out of infant's crib.
- Keep toys belonging to older children away from infants and toddlers.
- Remove drawstrings from children's clothing. They can cause a child to strangle if caught on a toy or play equipment.

Falls

- Use acceptable gates across stairways.
- Windows and balconies should be secured on every floor. Install window guards, if necessary.
- Infants should never be left on a bed or any elevated surface, even for a second.

Home Security

- Doors leading outside should be locked securely, especially in homes of toddlers or preschoolers.
- Always know where the children are and check on them frequently.
- Never open the door to a stranger.
- Always refuse entry to any "serviceman" whose visit is unexpected.
- Report to police any unusual incidents, strangers loitering around neighborhood or anything suspicious.
- Do not engage in conversation with telephone solicitors or with anyone who you do not know, even if they claim to be a relative.
- Even when expecting a service person, ask for credentials before letting him or her in, and if any doubt exists, refuse entry. Secure door and call to verify the serviceperson's identity with his/her employer (or yours).

EMERGENCY INFORMATION
911

MOTHER'S NAME_____ FATHER'S_____

FATHER'S WORK # _____ CELL # _____

MOTHER'S WORK#_____ CELL # _____

POISON CONTROL #_____

(If ever in doubt—always call & ask questions)

PEDIATRICIAN NAME_____TELEPHONE_____

   ADDRESS_____

ALTERNATE'S NAME _____TELEPHONE_____

HOSPITAL_____**EMERGENCY ROOM #**_____

(if ever in doubt about the seriousness of an injury—call for advice)

AMBULANCE_____#_____

(In an emergency,call an ambulance, especially if you have more than one child to care for)

DENTIST: NAME_____#_____

   ADDRESS_____

CLOSEST RELATIVE_____#_____

NEAREST NEIGHBOR_____#_____

MEDICAL INSURANCE_____#_____

   SUBSCRIBER #_____GROUP #_____

DENTAL INSURANCE_____#_____

SUBSCRIBER #_____GROUP #_____

FIRE SAFETY

Fire still remains the cause of many deaths and permanent injuries each year in the United States. Nannies must know the principles of fire safety and should teach them to their charges.

PRINCIPLES OF FIRE SAFETY:

1. <u>*Smoke Detectors:*</u> **Should be on each level of the home in hallways and <u>not in bedrooms.</u>**
   Know how the smoke detector works. Does it beep when batteries are low? How do you know it's in good working order? Extra batteries for smoke detectors should be on hand at all times.

2. <u>*Fire Extinguisher*</u>
   The home may have different kinds of extinguishers for different kinds of fires. Be certain you know what kind of fire the fire extinguisher you have is for. Some fire extinguishers can be used for almost any kind of fire. Be sure you know what is on hand before it is needed.
   Fire extinguishers are for small fires, not large ones, and children should always be removed from a home before you attempt to put out a fire in the event it gets out of control. Remember, children have been known to hide when a fire breaks out, and you can't watch them and fight a fire at the same time.
   Read the directions on the extinguisher and memorize them before you need to use it. This should be part of your drill.
   Ask your local fire department or a fire extinguisher about service and maintenance, especially after use.

3. <u>*Fuse Box*</u>
   - Know where the fuse box is in your employer's home.
   - Ask to be shown how to change a fuse or switch off the power.

4. <u>*Water Main*</u>
   Know where the water main turns on/off and how to use it.

5. *Plan a Fire Escape*
   - Draw the floor plan for each room in the house.
   - Remember "EDITH." It means: Escape Drills In The Home.
   - Label the exits on your drawing (1) door to hall, and (2) window to porch.
   - Each room should have two or more exits.
   - Rooms above first level should have access to specially designed "fire ladders" if the second exit is a window without a roof to climb onto.
   - Each room should be drawn and labeled with an explanation of which exit to use and any special instructions, e.g., fire ladder, escape.

6. *Meeting Place*
   Designate a place in the yard away from the house where everyone will meet to count heads in case of fire. There have been many instances where family members have reentered a burning house in search of a family member and died of smoke inhalation in the process, not knowing the person was already out of the house.

7. *Practice Fire Drills*
   In addition to teaching valuable (and perhaps live-saving) safety lessons, children find this to be fun. You can capitalize on the spirit of camaraderie while accomplishing an important responsibility at the same time. Drills should be practiced twice a month in different parts of the house.
   - All children from the age of two should learn how to "stop, drop and roll." If your clothes catch on fire, DO NOT RUN, as that will only fuel the flames. Rather, stop, drop to the floor or ground and roll over until the flames are extinguished. Remember: stop, drop and roll.
   - Practice feeling the highest part of the door you can reach. In the event of a fire, the top of the door would be hot and you would need to use the second exit documented on your fire escape plan.

- Be certain second exits are understood and operable, e.g., windows should open easily and exit ladders should be easily manipulated by children.
- Children should be taken out first since they may panic if you go first in the event of a real fire. As mentioned earlier, children have been known to hide when a fire has broken out because they become frightened.
- Practice and teach children what to do in the event of being unable to get out either exit e.g.
- Close doors between the fire/smoke and you. Closed doors will prevent smoke from pouring into the area you are in.
- Cover cracks at bottoms of doors, etc. with clothing or anything that will keep smoke out.
- Cover or close all vents to the room.
- If available, use the phone to call 911 to let the fire station know your exact whereabouts in the house.
- Have children memorize 911 or your local emergency response phone number and the exact address of the house.
- Since heat and smoke rise, practice crawling along the floor to prevent smoke inhalation, which is the leading cause of death in a fire, not burns.

Assess Home for Fire Safely Hazards as Part of the Fire Drill

- Frayed or otherwise damaged electrical cords are dangerous and must be replaced.
- Overuse of extension cords.
- Running extension cords under rugs or heavy furniture.
- Accumulation of debris, newspapers, rags, etc.
- Curling irons and other appliances left on.
- Matches or lighters left where children have access to them.
- Appliances left plugged in when not in use, e.g., coffee maker, etc.

Plan a Visit to Your Local Fire Station

Children enjoy this and it is educational as well. Bring a copy of your fire exit plan to the fire station with you and ask one of the fire fighters to evaluate it and make comments. This will help impress upon your charges how very serious the subject of fire safety is. While visiting the fire station ask about getting some "tot-finder" stickers for children's windows that alert fire fighters to areas of the house where children may be. You can usually get fire prevention information for children at your local fire department. Be sure to ask.

DEVELOPMENT OF FIRE EXIT PLAN

This assignment must include the number of rooms including children's bedrooms (ask parents before entering their bedroom!) You must name the exits for each room; each should have two. You must document if the home is equipped with fire extinguishers, where they are located and what kind of extinguisher they are. Document if the home is equipped with smoke detectors, where they are located and if more are needed. Also, document if any should be moved to a better location. You may feel free to call the local fire department for information if necessary. They are most willing to be helpful.

Note if children's rooms have "Tot-Finder" stickers on the windows. If not, did you discuss this idea with the parents? For age-appropriate children, initiate discussions with parents about practicing fire drills. Document the "meeting place."

FIRE
ESCAPE PLAN

Making and practicing a fire escape plan can save lives when a fire breaks out. Most people die from smoke, not flames or heat.

This four part plan could save your life!

1.   Install smoke detectors; Keep them in good working order

2.   Plan your escape route on a floor plan; decide on an outside meeting place

3.   Discuss this with your   family; decide who will take charge of a child if a fire occurs.

4.   Practice your exit plan, Especially at night

Use this grid or graph paper to draw a floor plan of each persons bedroom or to show the whole house

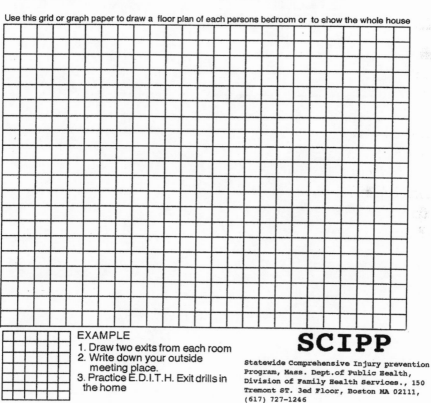

EXAMPLE
1. Draw two exits from each room
2. Write down your outside meeting place.
3. Practice E.D.I.T.H. Exit drills in the home

SCIPP

Statewide Comprehensive Injury prevention Program, Mass. Dept.of Public Health, Division of Family Health Services., 150 Tremont ST. 3ed Floor, Boston MA 02111, (617) 727-1246

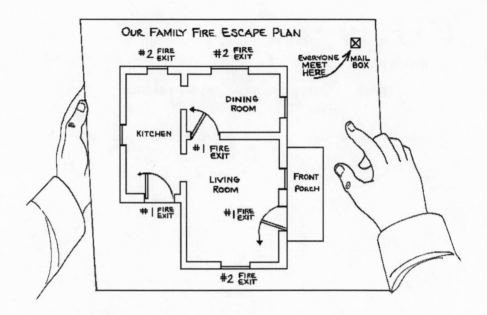

SAFETY STATISTICS

* 350 drowning deaths occur each year.
* Within a 3-year period, 67 children drowned in buckets. (CPSC 7/89)
* 350 children die each year choking on a piece of a toy. (NSC)
* Every year 130,000 children are treated at hospitals because of toy-related injuries.
* The Consumer Product Safety Commission does not and cannot test the 150,000 toys that go on the market every year.
* 250 infants died from suffocation/entrapment in the U.S. between 1985 and 1991.
* Injuries are the leading cause of death and disability among children. Injuries are not accidents; they are preventable and predictable.
* 55 deaths occur yearly from medicine or household cleaners.
* 34 deaths, 3,800 injuries occur yearly as a result of burns/scalding from hot water.
* 834 bicyclists were killed in crashes with motor vehicles in 1991 (none wore helmets—86% of the fatalities were the result of injuries to head).
* 140,000 injuries as a result of skateboard accidents in one-year (10-14 year-olds ranked the highest in incidence of injuries). (CPSC)
* 5,749 teenagers died in car accidents in 1991.
* More than 500,000 fires in the U.S. each year result in 6,000 deaths and 130,000 serious injuries.

PAMPHLETS

Home/Environmental Safety

Your Home Safety Checklist
National Safety Council, 1121 Spring Lake Dr., Itasca, IL 60143-3201.
Send $1 for each pamphlet. Visit their website at www.nsc.org

Preventing Accidental Poisonings
National Safety Council, 1121 Spring Lake Dr., Itasca, IL 60143-3201.
Send $1 for each pamphlet.

Home Safety Checklist
American Academy of Pediatrics, Publications Department,
P.O. Box 747 Elk Grove Village, IL 60009.

Poison Lookout Checklist
U.S. Consumer Product Safety Commission
Washington, DC 20207.

Locked Up Poisons
U.S. Consumer Product Safety Commission
Washington, DC 20207.

Child Safety Seat Package
U.S. Department of Transportation, National Highway Traffic Safety Administration,
400 Seventh St. SW, Washington, DC 20590. Visit their website at www.nhtsa.dot.gov

What You Need to Know About Airbags
Automotive Coalition for Traffic Safety, Inc., 1110 N. Glebe Rd. Ste. 1020, Arlington, VA 22201-4795. The first 2 pamphlets are free. Each

additional pamphlet is $.15. Visit their website at www.actsinc.org or call 703-243-7501 for additional information.

Preventing Rollovers, Crashes and Injuries
Automotive Coalition for Traffic Safety, Inc., 1110 N. Glebe Rd. Ste. 1020, Arlington, VA 22201-4795. The first 2 pamphlets are free. Each additional pamphlet is $.15.

These pamphlets are free unless otherwise noted.

CHAPTER SEVEN

Growth & Development
Erikson and Developmental Psychology

Erik Homberger Erikson's theory is based on the model that individuals pass through eight developmental stages beginning at birth. According to Erikson, each stage of a person's development has its own agenda, a task to be performed and a goal to be achieved. Each stage is built upon the one preceding it. Each is the foundation for accomplishing the task in the stages that follow. It is generally accepted that from birth to approximately seven years of age, the child's development is most malleable, and certainly the most critical period of development, having a profound effect on the rest of our lives.

There is a timetable for each stage of development, and regardless of whether or not we have reached our goal in each stage, we nevertheless move on to the next. When a goal in any particular stage is not achieved, however, the subsequent stages become more difficult to navigate. As we look at the earliest stages, it will become apparent how the Nanny can either enhance or hinder the psychological progress of the developing child.

Being able to attain the goal of each stage depends on various factors. There is belief among experts that genetics may play an important role in determining whether or not the child reaches his or her goals in any particular stage. However, for our purposes, we will be concerned about how the care a child receives influences the achievement of the child's goals in each of the most critical stages of development.

From a practical perspective, most Nannies realize they are more adept working with toddlers than adolescents, for example. Or perhaps we prefer infants or school-agers to toddlers. Whatever age with which you are most comfortable is fine—the important thing is to know which it is. This is a vital piece of knowledge for both the Nanny and the parent. Whether or not the child is successful in any particular stage has much to do with how the child's caregiver responds to the child's needs in that particular stage.

The following reflects Erikson's eight stages of development.

STAGE 1—HOPE: Trust vs. Mistrust (Infancy)

During infancy, 0-15 months, the task for the child is to develop a sense of hope. In order for the infant to develop a sense of hope, there is a need to be well cared for and feel that the world is a safe, comfortable place. The child who is successful in this first critical stage is a child whose needs are met promptly and with loving care. As the child becomes used to being nurtured (e.g., fed before there is a need to scream to get attention to be fed, held before there is a need to cry for attention, and kept warm without having to bellow in discomfort), the infant will come to trust the surrounding environment and the developmental task is achieved as the infant develops a sense of hope about his existence.

It is clear from the preceding examples that the Nanny who anticipates the infant's needs, is responsive, freely nurturing, and generally committed to the infant enhances the child's development and helps the infant achieve its goal. Alternatively, when the infant is hungry, cold or in pain development is hindered and the infant's goal is not achieved. The environment is distrusted and the infant is often irritable or withdrawn.

According to Erikson, if the infant achieves the goal of developing a sense of hope about its existence at this early stage, the ability to be hopeful through life is enhanced. If the goal of developing hope is achieved, the infant will feel safe and will trust others through life, allowing the infant to transit easily to the next stage of development.

STAGE 2—WILL: Autonomy vs. Shame, Doubt (Early Childhood)

The task of the next stage is the development of a "will." Also known as the "terrible twos," this is the stage from about fifteen months to approximately two years, nine months. While this stage of development is one of exploration, and the drive to explore is strong, it is potentially dangerous if the environment is not made safe for the child's explorations. Many people believe that the child in this stage of development is a rebel. "Willful," "stubborn" and "determined" are descriptive words of this stage. The child is not really rebelling, but rather trying to satisfy his or her newfound intense curiosity of the world. Therefore, the child's desire to seek and explore must be nurtured in order for the task to be completed.

Making the environment safe for the exploring child provides opportunities for the child to investigate and discover. In days gone by, children in this stage were restrained and considered "terrible" because of their normal desire to explore, which ultimately got them into trouble. Today, we understand the developmental process and encourage the child. We make the environment safe; we encourage inquisitiveness; we provide stimulation. We refrain from smothering the child who seems to have made the transition overnight from our affectionate little snuggler to a pint-size steamroller with an agenda of his or her own. The type of Nanny needed is someone who will encourage the child's developing sense of autonomy, yet who is ever-present thus providing a sense of security. It is typical for the child to run off to play, returning frequently to "check in" as there is a need to know you will still be there.

STAGE 3—PURPOSE: Initiative vs. Guilt (Play Age)

The preschooler's task is to develop a sense of who he or she is as an individual, and the development of the ability to assert oneself. The child, seeing that significant others in his life are separate individuals, is figuring out that everyone is composed of many facets with differing roles and purposes—multifaceted individuals.

Discovering various personal aspects, the child likes to put ideas out there as a way of getting feedback from significant others. Often, children in this stage will identify part of themselves with a creature who is strong and scary to others by saying such things as "I am Terrace, the fierce tiger." The proper response is something along the lines of "Hello Terrace, I hope you've already eaten," thereby validating the child's sense of power.

The child is establishing his own understanding of his individual personality traits and needs to know that all parts of him are accepted. It is possible in this stage to hinder development by discrediting a part of the child's individuality. We do this when we disapprove of a particular aspect of the child's personality, such as when we say (with facial expressions, words or indifference) that the more sensitive part of his or her nature should not be acted out.

This is the time when society and the roles we place on the sexes can have impact. What the child needs is approval of all the feelings, ideas and roles with which he or she wishes to experiment. Should your little boy want to play dress-up and try his sister's make-up, it has nothing whatsoever to do with his future gender preference. This kind of role-playing can be disturbing to adults who do not have an understanding of normal child development, and the disapproval of the adult can result in the child feeling guilty and ashamed, thus hindering development. This exercise in trying out different roles from wanting to be a tiger to wanting to be a ballerina is merely explorative. It is wise to keep in mind that the child should be encouraged to experiment with his or her imagination in this way. All identities are being integrated into what will become the child's own unique self.

We enhance development when we show our acceptance of all of the various characteristics that are emerging. We will see the children in this stage acting out the roles of mothers and fathers and see them taking the initiative in these roles. For instance, a child will want to push a play lawn mower behind the parent mowing the lawn. Perhaps the child will want to help by washing the dishes. These initiatives may be inconvenient—and also, messy. However, encouraging this behavior in spite of the inconvenience or mess will help the child learn that it is right and beneficial to experiment.

This is the basis for individualization, forming an identity and a strong sense of self and purpose. It is the basis for the ability to assert oneself later in life and take the initiative.

STAGE 4—COMPETENCE: Industry vs. Inferiority (School Age)

This next stage of development begins around the time the child begins elementary school. If all has gone fairly well, the child now wants to test personal power and its limits. This is the last critical stage of early development. As the child tests the effect and impact of this power on family and friends, their responses will determine feelings of competence and level of self-esteem. Initiative, aggressiveness and competitiveness are all characteristics of this stage. The child needs to know in as positive a way as possible, the boundaries of assertiveness and/or aggressiveness.

The child has a serious investment in being "right," winning games, completing tasks, and receiving approval from significant adults. This industriousness is healthy and normal in spite of the fact that the child may appear to be aggressive. Care should be taken with little girls that they not be made to feel un-feminine, or otherwise inferior as a result of their natural desire to compete and express their personal power. As with every stage of development, the Nanny should be vigilant against any conditioned responses of a sexist nature that they may possess. For example, comments such as "Little girls don't act that way" are never appropriate because it implies that little boys may. The aggressive and competitive behaviors we see at this stage are not necessarily indications that the child will always display such tendencies. In fact, it is important to keep in mind at every stage of your child's development that what you see in the child is not "the finished product." Parents, more so than Nannies, sometimes tend to look at the child's behavior in terms of "what kind of a person has my child become?" It is useful to remember and to remind the parent that in most cases the behaviors we see in a child's early development are NOT a reflection of who the child will eventually "become." Children are always learning, growing and developing. What is needed when aggressive behavior is encountered is gentle limit setting that addresses the behavior, rather than admonishment, which leaves the child feeling guilty.

Ironically, it is when a child is made to feel guilty, inferior, or helpless with regard to power that trying to prove that power may become ingrained. Children at this stage need to be validated, affirmed and recognized for their sense of industry and desire to become competent. Negative behaviors are best discouraged when the significant adult spends time modeling behavior and talking about what is appropriate and what is not. Frequent non-evaluative praise is essential.

During elementary school years, the child is developing a sense of social competence broadening the interpersonal arena to include peer groups. It is within the framework of relationships with peers that the child develops a sense of cooperation and concern for others.

It is necessary now for the child to form attachments with a peer or peers while figuring out how to be autonomous within the peer group, establish a separate identity, and then feel competent among peers. In some ways these transitions are a repetition of the first four stages of the child's early development—Hope, Will, Purpose and Competence. Now, however, the child is experiencing these transitions in the world— in a peer/social context—as opposed to a limited family setting.

Needed now is adult help in the form of teaching social skills. During this phase the child is learning compassion and empathy for peers. It is important to assist the child in facilitating social life logistics while at the same time allowing as much space as the child needs to operate independently. Allowing the child to decide who he does and does not want to spend time with, encouraging him to call friends on the phone to make plans as well as raising his consciousness with regard to social skills, are all part of the Nanny's responsibility when caring for a school-age child. It is also important to be respectful of the child's choice of friends. As peers mirror the child's image, the approval and willingness of the adult to include the child's friends on outings and visits sends a message that the child possesses the ability to function and be successful socially.

STAGE 5—FIDELITY:
Identity vs. Identity Confusion (Adolescence)

Adolescence is a period of time that begins in the middle-school years and can continue well into a person's twenties, and perhaps even beyond that.

When a child lacks a strong emotional connection to a significant adult, adolescence is marked by greater identity confusion and the delay of the development of fidelity. The development of fidelity involves first and foremost, fidelity to oneself. A prerequisite for this is self-awareness. In order to possess self-awareness, the developing adolescent must have trusted role models who can communicate authentically and with whom he or she can relate.

When this occurs, the adolescent can relate to ideals, beliefs and standards of human behavior. Thus, the child's identity is formed around beliefs that are held most valuable. Only when adolescents can believe in and commit to personal standards, values and ideals will they be capable of knowing who they are and in what they believe. Once identity has taken root, the adolescent is capable of fidelity personally and in relationships with others. In order for development to progress to where the adolescent becomes a young adult capable of intimacy, the goal of fidelity must be realized.

STAGE 6—LOVE: Intimacy vs. Isolation (Young Adulthood)

First and foremost, when we refer to intimacy in the context of human growth and development, we refer to the young adult's ability to be EMOTIONALLY intimate. Although physical intimacy is an important part of adult relationships, it soon becomes empty if we are not capable of emotional intimacy. Emotional intimacy involves the ability to communicate our feelings freely and authentically. Intimacy is not possible without first having established an identity since, if we do not know who we are and what we believe in, how are we able to discuss and act on those feelings with a partner? The achievement of intimacy is necessary for a fruitful marriage and close friendships. Intimacy demands the ability to move toward the other not simply for one's own gain, but out of love. There is always a risk in such a move: the risk of being absorbed by the other. This is why intimacy is so often feared. The opposite of intimacy is distancing, which often leads to a sense of isolation and a manipulative relationship to others. The absence of intimacy often leads to an ongoing demand for unconditional love without reciprocity.

ADULT DEVELOPMENT

MIDDLE AGE

In your role as a Nanny it is likely many of the people you come in contact with will be in the middle age period. In our culture, middle age brings about in us deep anxieties about decline and dying. For some, there is a fear that after youth there is no life. Some people believe that to be over 30 is to be "over the hill." Negative images of old age lead to fears without foundations about the "middle years." Yet each stage in the life cycle has its own virtues and limitations.

The middle ages sometimes bring with them a variety of changes. For some, there is a loss of youthful vitality, of energy and drive. These changes often are experienced as a fundamental threat. The "middle age crisis" is felt when the adult begins to sense her own mortality.

The term generativity is of special importance in this stage. Generativity is demonstrated by assuming responsibility for young adult's in the following ways:

- Assisting teenage children to become responsible and happy adults.
- Achieving adult social and civic responsibility.
- Reaching and maintaining satisfactory performance in one's career.
- Developing adult leisure time activities.
- Adjusting to aging parents.

The generative person contains within himself a fund or basic trust in the world and hope for the future. This trust gives the generative person the possibility of grasping that the negative dimensions of life are real yet will not in the end outweigh the positive. This basic trust and hope generates the sense that one's life has made a difference. The generative person can accept the ups and downs, the positive, and the negative aspects of life while valuing the process.

The opposite of generativity is stagnation, not growing, being stuck, or perhaps feeling bogged down in a life full of obligation and lacking self-fulfillment.

This is a period when the previous accomplishments come into question: "What have I done with my life? What have I done to make a difference in this world?, How will I be remembered?, What are my goals now and what do I want to do with the rest of my life?,

The mid-life transition can truly be a time of real crisis.

Chart A		
MID-LIFE ADJUSTMENTS		
Potential Losses	Potential Losses	Potential Gains
Health and strength	Cognitive capacities	Maturity, experience
Hearing and vision	Old learning	Frustration tolerance
Appearance and body image	Long-term memory	Cautiousness
Reaction time	Immediate memory	Accuracy
Psychomotor skills	Work productivity	Need for achievement
Employment	Personality traits	Adaptability
Independence, identity	Creativity	Work morale, loyalty
Sense of usefulness	Sexuality	Less supervision
Time structure	Social awareness	Fewer job accidents
Social status	Nurturance	Lower absenteeism
Parent, spouse	Estheticism	Lower quit rate
Children, friends	Coping mechanisms	Higher job satisfaction
Involvement (engagement)	Sense of well being	More free time
Income	Responsibility, reliability	

THE DEVELOPMENT TASKS OF OLD AGE

Old age is a difficult period of life for us to understand, not only because it is a distinctive stage in the life cycle but also because it is uniquely oriented to the now. Its sense of "newness" is different from the sense of time in youth, middle age or early old age. Because there is no promise of years yet to be lived, the future does not have the power to justify the present moment as in youth or middle age.

It is important for the Nanny to have a basic understanding of the elderly since she may be interacting with her charges' grandparents (employers parents) as integral family members.

Society offers little understanding of our support for this sense of "now" in old age. As a result, younger persons do not move through life with high expectation for old age.

Most elderly are not in nursing homes, nor are they abandoned by their families. In fact, family members now provide eighty percent of the care giving for older adults in this country. Conditions of life for many elderly are now better than in the past thanks to Social Security, pension plans, and medicate. As a result most elderly can expect a longer, healthier and more fulfilled life. Yet our culture retains negative images of the aging process. It is not unusual for young adults to declare that they would rather die than grow old. Elderly men and women facing serious problems associated with advancing age, prefer to go it alone instead of taking advantage of resources to which they are entitled because they feel that life would no longer be worthwhile if they were to become dependent on others for their needs. Since fear of dependency weighs heavily upon both old and young, there is a real need to address these fears.

What governs our attitude toward the aging in America is an ideology that has been described as ageism. Ageism is a form of discrimination that is comparable to racism and to sexism. It involves a process of systematic stereotyping the elderly as dependant, frail, senile, forgetful, no longer useful to society, and in general a burden.

The older adult's attitude towards dependency is negative; it leads to the experience of self-worthlessness and self-loss. In America, the possibility of facing old age with dignity is destroyed from the outside, from a culture that considers old age as a period of irretrievable loss and decline, although this attitude is slowly changing as older people become more aware of health and fitness.

During these later years individuals are faced with tasks that are unique to their developmental stage. This time in life is a period of reaming. It is a period of facing new and unresolved problems rather than a period of floating gently on the surface of familiar solutions to familiar problems. In addition to continuing human needs such as the need for emotional security and affection, the need for social recognition and status—the need for maintenance of worth and self respect are very important. Older people seem to learn to cope with a number of developmental concerns such as the following:

- Death of a spouse and friends.
- Retirement and a reduced income.
- Reduced physical vigor.
- Changed living arrangements.
- Singular affiliation within an age group of elders.
- Development of new leisure time so that it will be constructive and satisfying.
- Caring for an aged body.
- The need to develop new social roles that can result in recognition and respect.
- Making satisfactory living arrangements.
- Making new friends.
- Treating grown children as adults.

Also, the older person frequently fears becoming physically or mentally helpless, becoming economically insecure, being rejected by society and suffers particular insults of the aging process such as loss of physical attractiveness, lessening of physical health, and loss of social status. It is important to mention here though, that more and more of the older population has taken a proactive approach to old age.

All of these demand that the older person be an efficient learner. With the exception of early childhood, demands for development of coping skills are greater on the older person than during any other period of life.

CHAPTER EIGHT

High Self-Esteem and the Developing Child

High self-esteem has been described as that "resilient inner core," or as that "emotional hardiness" that some children seem to possess naturally. These are the children who bounce back from the disappointments that can emotionally cripple others.

Our level of self-esteem permeates all of our life choices, from how well we take care of ourselves to how well we care for and relate to others. The amount of self-esteem we either possess or lack determines our everyday outlook on life, how we respond in a crisis, and the quality and satisfaction we gain in our relationships. The level of self-esteem affects the child's grades in school, whom the child chooses for friends and how easily the child makes and sustains those friendships. Experts know that children who have adequate self-esteem are much less likely to develop drug or alcohol problems, and are more likely to be hopeful, have a positive attitude, pursue interests and attend college.

Knowing this, it becomes obvious that helping the child build high self-esteem should most certainly be a priority anytime one is concerned about growth and development. High self-esteem is nurtured not by providing the best in material things, but instead by maintaining emotional connection with the child. After all is said and done, it basically comes down to being sincerely interested in spending time with the child. In fact, spending time with the child is the only way of maintaining the strong emotional connection.

Each of us makes a silent statement about what matters most to us by the amount of time we spend attending to a particular endeavor. This is true whether it is a job, a hobby, or a relationship. We all have our priorities. Intuitively children know this. In Scott Beck's *The Road Less Traveled*, there is an essay in section II entitled "The Work of Attention." This essay discusses the effort and value of simply listening to a child. It is a profound illustration of how simple, yet how difficult it is to fully appreciate our children.

Children with high self-esteem tend to come from environments where there is a real commitment on the part of significant adults to the developing child. In these nurturing relationships the child is aware that he or she is a priority in the lives of the significant adults as opposed to a chore with which the adult has to deal. The child feels the love and respect of the adult. Interestingly, the children with fewer material things are many times the children with the highest self-esteem. This may be because these children do not have the same need for objects to occupy their time, perhaps because of a strong sense of family and a sense of satisfaction about life in general. We live in a society where, for many parents, there is a striving and an urgency to give our children "the best" in material things. For other parents, there may be a sense of disappointment at not being able to provide all of the material things the children might wish to have. It is ironic that the most valuable gift we can bestow on a child is the gift of self-esteem, which no amount of money can buy.

LEARNING STYLES

A primary responsibility of the Nanny is to observe and honor the inherent nature of those in one's care, developing management skills to suit the needs of each child with keen attention to environmental influences. In order to foster a positive environment, a place of maximum comfort where self-esteem flourishes, the Nanny must learn how and when to acknowledge and appreciate different personality types with utmost respect. With attention to preferential learning styles, there are many ways to guide and enhance the child's natural abilities to maximize potential for growth and excellence.

It is important to respect individual learning styles to foster positive self worth. Provisions should be made with regard to:

- Children who prefer to play and work with other children.
- Children who prefer to work alone.
- Children who like help getting started on a new activity.
- Children who prefer help on request.
- Children who prefer action or people oriented activities.
- Children who prefer working by themselves with objects.

Although all children should be supported in their preferred learning styles, they should also be encouraged to try new ways of interacting with people and materials.

Getting to know the personality type of the child is crucial for the development of healthy self-esteem. Knowing and appreciating the child's particular nature will enable the Nanny to understand individual style and strengths to maximize success in enhancing the child's sense of self worth. The following chart is adapted from "People Types and Tiger Stripes" from the publication *A Practical Guide to Learning Styles*, by Gordon Lawrence.

Extroverts
- Enjoy talk, movement, action, learning
- Enjoy cooperative projects
- Readily share and speak in groups
- Want to experience things to really understand them

Sensing Types
- Learn best in step by step progression
- Enjoy structure
- Value the practical
- Excel at memory tasks
- Good with details/knows the overall routine

Thinking Types
- Need logistical rational for projects
- More truthful than tactful
- Wants fairness more than harmony
- Able to be objective
- Takes facts and ideas seriously

Judging Types
- Decisive and organized
- Good at completing tasks

Introverts
- Think, plan and rehearse before sharing ideas
- Enjoy solitary reading, writing
- Can work for long periods on one project
- May spend a great deal of time thinking about something before actually doing it

Intuitive Types
- Prefer concepts to discrete facts
- Excel at Imaginative tasks
- Tend to avoid details
- Readily grasps words and symbols
- Impatient with routine/need to be predictable

Feeling Types
- Need personal encouragement —the human angle
- Allow feelings to override logic and objectivity
- Suppress needs and Ideas to keep harmony
- Able to be empathetic
- Dislike being contrary

Perceiving Types
- Flexible and curious, but tend to procrastinate
- Start too much and may finish too little
- Need to prioritize and Improve decision-making skills

THE VERBAL ENVIRONMENT

Probably the most insidious and prevalent factor in whether or not the child possesses high self-esteem has to do with the verbal environment e.g. the way that family members talk to one another. Although the ability to communicate well can play a huge role in enhancing self-esteem, it does not in any way guarantee that the verbal environment is free of the subtle nuances that either make or break the developing child's sense of worth.

The obvious blocks to the development of high self-esteem (name calling, sarcasm, and passive-aggressive communication styles) are not what we are talking about here. In fact, not only are these styles destructive to the developing child, but also to the adult with average self-esteem who will suffer if living in an environment where there are consistent subtle put-downs.

Subtle components of the verbal environment include words and silence such as how much adults say, how well they listen, the tone of voice used, and to whom they talk. Examples of common negative adult behaviors include:

- Adult is in a hurry, shows little or no interest in the child's activities.
- Adult pays superficial attention to what the child has to say.
- Adult speaks discourteously to the child, interrupts, speaks to the child in a demanding, Impatient or belligerent manner.
- Adult uses judgmental vocabulary in describing child to self and others, e.g., "hyper," "stubborn," etc.
- Adult relies on giving orders or making demands as the predominant means of interaction.
- Adults asks questions for which no real answer is expected or can be given, e.g., "What do you think you're doing?" or "When will you ever learn?".

Few adults and certainly those who care for children as their profession would intentionally create a negative verbal environment. However, it is, unfortunately, a common occurrence in many settings. We get busy and don't think about the impact our words have. We don't think before we speak because we're not used to stopping and thinking about how we are coming across. Positive verbal environments usually don't happen by chance. They are intentionally implemented by thoughtful, caring adults who want the best for the children in their care.

Here are some common non-empathetic responses that contribute to feelings of low self-worth in children (from Diane Loomans "Full Esteem Ahead"). They convey the message that the child's feelings are unimportant or not acceptable. The child may then internalize the message: "I am not important or acceptable."

- SHAMING: "Stop that ridiculous fussing! Do you want our company to think you are a baby?" (Result: The child is judged and labeled and may feel anger or shame.)
- DISCOUNTING: "There's nothing to be sad about. You're blowing this way out of proportion. Dry those tears right now." (Result: The child's feelings are discounted, and the child is likely to feel frustrated, angry or doubt his or her own feelings and reality.)
- DISTRACTING: "Come on, let's play with the dog until the company arrives." (Result: The child is distracted and may feel puzzled or confused.)
- BARGAINING: "If you're polite while the company is here, I'll take you for some ice cream later." (Result: The child is likely to feel confused or frustrated.)
- THREATENING: "I'll give you something really to cry about if you don't stop that nonsense!" (Result: The child is threatened with violence, and most likely feels scared or angry.)

- SHUNNING: "Go to your room and stay there. I don't want to talk to you or see you when you act this way." (Result: The child is isolated and may feel lonely, scared or sad.)

Through practice and conscious attention, the Nanny can learn to avoid these common techniques and replace them with a positive and productive approach.

Marshall Rosenberg, Ph.D., the international peacemaker and founder of the Center for Nonviolent Communication in Cleveland, Ohio, has created a simple model to follow for effectively communicating with compassion. Listening with compassion and empathy strengthens our connection with children and minimizes the likelihood of creating a defensive or detrimental reaction. It is important to establish a safe way to resolve conflict, where one is comfortable even though vulnerable, and where one is free to express feelings without judgment.

The use of the "I" messages creates an atmosphere of understanding and mutual respect.

Structure	Example
I feel (State of Emotion)	angry
When you (State of Emotion)	leave your clothes on the bathroom floor.
Because (State the effect of the behavior)	it's embarrassing when I have people visiting.
And I would like (State the specific behavior)	to have the house look neat.

In addition to using this format for empathetic listening, here are some everyday communication tips that contribute to positive self-esteem:

COMMUNICATION TIPS FOR POSITIVE SELF-ESTEEM

- Say "Good Job" and "I knew you could do it."
- Ask, "What's wrong?" Let children know their feelings are important. Work out problems together.
- Pick them up when they're down. Remind them that one mistake doesn't mean they're not smart or capable. Make time to help them learn so that they can succeed the next time.
- When they ask a question, answer it right away. Don't be afraid to say, "I don't know." Look up answers together.

The key to effective communication is patience and understanding. In a typical day, the Nanny is challenged by many different situations that require on the spot responses. By becoming familiar with personality types, active listening skills, and constructive communication, the esteem of the Nanny is improved to the benefit of the children. Learning to pause, to take a deep breath before responding, can help the Nanny implement the best possible action for any given event. If mistakes are made, review them in a non-judgmental way. Think of how the situation might have been handled more effectively, make the necessary amends, and let go of the blame. It can be helpful to visualize familiar scenarios to see yourself reacting in a manner that would promote the most positive outcome. Remember, it is perfectly acceptable to apologize anytime you react in a way that is less than desirable. By doing so you are teaching children how to be authentic (honest,) showing them how to apologize and that everyone makes mistakes.

EVALUATIVE VERSUS NON-EVALUATIVE PRAISE

As we have come to respect the child's need for truthfulness, it is easy to understand why the difference between evaluative versus non-evaluative praise is so important.

Evaluative praise includes statements such as, "You are terrific," "You are the best baseball player on your team," or "What a fantastic artist you are."

The problem with evaluative praise is that it attaches a superlative quality that: a) can't always be lived up to, and b) is void of specific authenticity. It becomes a problem almost immediately when the child feels that this is now the standard to uphold. The problem with evaluative praise, and the reason why it is called "evaluative," is that no one is always "fantastic," "the best," or "terrific." This kind of praise evaluates the results of the child's effort, and it follows that if the child does not perform as well next time, that somehow he or she is not quite up-to-par. Another problem with evaluative praise is that after a while it begins to sound thoughtless and empty because the superlatives don't include reference to anything that actually took place, such as effort, tenacity or improvement.

PRAISE THE ACT—Rather than falling into the trap of using evaluative praise, which is what we have been conditioned to use, be descriptive instead. Rather than saying "What a fantastic artist you are," say instead: "I really like the way you used the red and purple together—the sky looks so realistic."

An added benefit of this more thoughtful style of communication is that the child will begin to value the process involved in any particular effort, rather than always focusing on the results. This is critical if the child is ever to learn how to take risks in any kind of creative endeavor.

DESCRIBE, DESCRIBE, DESCRIBE—The key is to describe, describe and describe some more. This requires more thought on the part of the adult, but to the child it has the ring of authenticity. The child is not made to feel pressured to achieve a consistent and unreasonable standard of perfection or to be "the best." Children (and adults also, for that matter) can end up feeling inadequate when performance doesn't meet the standard set for themselves—the reality is: none of us can always be terrific. The result can actually be that the child's self-esteem suffers. Everyone should have the right to be imperfect, to make mistakes and to have bad days.

It can be extremely difficult to re-teach ourselves when it comes to evaluative vs. non-evaluative/descriptive praise. It takes practice and thoughtfulness. Here are some examples:

Evaluative	Non-Evaluative
"You're super at building."	"I noticed how you've learned to balance these blocks to make the building taller."
"You're an awesome baseball player."	"The play you made on second base shows "how much more coordinated you've become. Congratulations!"
"Wow, what a beautiful little girl you are."	"The warmth of your smile, along with your personality makes me feel good."
You're such a great kid."	"I'm so glad to be with you today, thanks for coming along."
"You are a super organizer."	"Thanks for picking up all of those little play mobile toys; it took a lot of patience on your part to get them all."

CHAPTER NINE

Curriculum & Creative Play

Curriculum

Children are absorbing knowledge and information in volumes every day—they are learning regardless of how much effort the adult puts into it. Curriculum is a term once reserved for teachers in classroom settings and involves assessing the needs of the child and planning activities which will encourage the child to learn and grow.

The role of the Nanny has changed and evolved over the past two decades, especially in the United States and as it has, parents have come to expect that the nanny will plan appropriate activities (curriculum) as part of the daily routine. Professional nannies are the private tutors of the children in their care, even if they have had no formal teacher training. For our purposes, the terms; curriculum, play plans & activities are interchangeable

The Process Is The Point

Nannies as early childhood educators must keep in mind one very important principle when planning curriculum. Regardless if it is art, building blocks, applying make-up for a dramatic play, or simply singing a song,

"The process is the point." Process, rather than content or the "end result" is what matters anytime we talk about being creative with children.

Imagine you are painting a picture. You are thinking of a scene you saw in a movie. You are engrossed in what you are doing as you add colors & objects to the painting someone comes along and asks, "What's that?" "A forest," you reply. To which the observer responds, "It doesn't look like a forest to me." This is, in fact, what happens to many children when adults or others expect them to be creative within a compartmentalized framework, or anytime a child's efforts are ridiculed.

The concept of taking risks and stretching creatively is limited any time we are looking for specific outcomes. When children are allowed to be creative in their playtime activities, such as when they paint or make up stories, the seeds are planted for creativity far beyond children's play. It is, in fact, the basis for becoming creative problem-solvers as children mature and later on in business and in relationships.

Wanting to find other ways to do things and feeling confident enough to explore the possibilities are characteristics that take root in childhood when we are encouraged to use our creative genius. The child who is cared for by adults who nurture the process of creativity stands a much better chance of success in the world than the child who approaches each creative endeavor with a specific outcome in mind.

It is part of the creative process to make allowances, and actually to encourage the absurd, the unusual and the ridiculous. It is perfectly appropriate to draw lips on ducks if that is what the child wants to do. Too many times, however, the adult will inhibit the child by saying something like, "You know that ducks don't have lips. Give him a bill instead" When we are drawing, we should not confuse the process with science. It is important to note that science has made great strides via individuals who were creative and open to all possibilities.

Perhaps the adult needs to understand that once children feel a sense of comfort with their creative risk-taking and can actually find humor in the absurd results of their efforts, they are able to approach other tasks with more confidence, knowing that the only limit they have is their own imagination. In any creative endeavor, adults should refrain from imposing structure and allow the child's imagination to determine the limits. When we do this, we are honoring the part of the child that is patient, industrious, colorful, able to maintain concentration, confident and spontaneous. These are all skills that are truly appreciated in the world of business as well as in any endeavor.

When we honor the <u>process</u>, we are looking at the <u>effort</u> the child expends, which means so much more in terms of satisfaction than the "end result" could command. It is in the <u>process</u> that children learn vital skills.

Certainly with school-age children there has to be more structure if, for instance you are assisting the child with a school project. There will be guidelines to follow and deadlines to meet. Academics require a certain outcomes usually measured by grades. The Nanny's role with school-age children is to look at all of the areas of human development in relation to the child and build a curriculum to enhance the areas that most need enhancement.

Structured vs. Unstructured Play

Structured play can be defined as playtime in which the Nanny is an active participant. Structured play is your opportunity to introduce the child to new ideas and concepts or to teach them sociable behavior, e.g., how to "take turns," etc. This is accomplished not only by interacting verbally, but also by organizing specific activities in which the child will engage independently while the Nanny supervises and participates occasionally e.g., filling a small tub with water and allowing a two year old to wash a doll while the Nanny prepares a shopping list etc. It is essential for the Nanny to be involved with the activity to the extent that help may be offered redirecting the child, if necessary, and to talk about what's going on.

There should be a balance between the amount of structured and unstructured time the child spends each day. Since you will be interacting with the child, structured playtime is the time when a child is most apt to be developing his or her own perception. It's important to talk about what is going on, and just as important for you to listen to what the child is communicating. Even if the child is pre-verbal you can pick up information via body language, e.g., boredom, pride. Anytime you have the opportunity to praise the child (including infants) you should do so—enthusiastically. The best way to praise is to comment on what is going on rather than resorting to "evaluative praise," e.g., "You are terrific," or "What a good boy you are." Instead say, "Wow, everything you build gets bigger. That shows your balance is improving." Review Chapter One for further information on evaluative vs. non-evaluative praise.

Unstructured Time

One of the major goals of parents and Nannies is to raise a child who can function independently. Unstructured playtime is one of the ways children learn to develop a sense of independence and how to be resourceful. However, it is still necessary to provide them with the proper materials for unstructured play. It may also be necessary from time to time to reinforce that by saying, "It's time to play by yourself for a while." Children naturally prefer to have someone share in their fun and enjoyment. It is not possible for any adult to spend their entire day, every day, totally immersed in play with them, nor would it be the best thing for the child even if it were possible.

Unstructured play can be defined as the time when the child is occupied with activities or interests that are not reliant upon the Nanny's participation, such as playing with an empty box, certain toys, books or any number of other things that will naturally amuse a child depending on age. The fine line between structured and unstructured play is maintained when the child is informed when the Nanny is or is not available to participate in the child's activities.

In general, children who participate in adequate amounts of meaningful interaction will easily adapt to situations where they must use their own resources to entertain themselves. What's important is a good balance between the two and to be perceptive to times when more of one than the other is needed

Toys are heavily employed during unstructured playtime. To prevent boredom from taking over, rotate toys so that all of the child's toys aren't available to play with all the time. Most children have more toys than they know what to do with and usually will not even notice if some of them are put away for a while. A good time to check them is while the child is napping or otherwise occupied. It is also a good opportunity for you to look them over and clean them. Toys brought out of the closet after a month or so are more interesting especially since they haven't been played with for a while. Naturally, you would not rotate a favorite stuffed animal or any other toy for which the child has a special affection.

Using television as an unstructured activity is not a good idea. The writers and producers of children's TV commercials have one goal in mind, and that is to convince children that they need to have whatever the commercial is selling. Furthermore, much of what is marketed to children has no value whatsoever. Many cartoons still contain violence that many children will imitate. Even the old Disney cartoons show characters kicking and hitting each other over the head. A two-year-old watches one character hit another and then the flattened victim jumps up and walks away. When the two-year-old imitates this using his 11-month-old brother as a victim, not only does he hurt his sibling, but he also gets himself into a lot of trouble. Other children who watch soap operas and other valueless programs are exposed to the redundant depiction of unhealthy adult relationships, which can have an effect on their developing values, especially if they watch frequently. Therefore, in general, television should NOT be used as an unstructured activity.

The other effect of being exposed to violence and unhealthy adult relationships via television is that the child's perception of the world and how people relate to each other can become tainted and negative. Some people may argue that exposure to real life events, violent or not, is a kind of reality orientation that children should be aware of and not protected from. A child will have plenty of opportunity to become familiar with the harsh realities of life without being introduced to them at home. It is necessary to make the young child's world as positive as possible. Positive and optimistic perceptions and attitudes are the necessary building blocks for problem solving skills that every individual needs in order to interact successfully throughout their lifetime.

The only time TV is valuable is when a program is chosen by an adult with the best interests of the developing and impressionable child in mind. TV programs should be watched together so that afterward both you and the child can talk about the program.

Educational Play

Although all play is educational to differing degrees, the term "educational play" is marketed to parents by manufacturers of children's products (toys, learning kits, etc). with the objective of capitalizing on every parent's desire to raise a successful competent child. Ironically, overzealous parents who push "educational play" on their children before they are ready may be instilling distaste for academics in the child as well as damaging the child's self-esteem. If the education is beyond the developmental capability of the child, a sense of failure is reinforced that may disrupt the child's natural inclination to learn. Obviously this is the last attitude any parent would want their child to develop regarding learning.

Therefore the term "educational play" in the commercial sense (products or programs) should be viewed with a certain amount of skepticism. Play is an integral part of development and learning occurs naturally. It is the Nanny's responsibility to provide the right atmosphere (enthusiasm) and some creative ideas to enhance the child's natural inclination to engage in meaningful play.

THE PLAY PLAN

Nannies and teachers plan curriculum/activities/play plans which address the developmental needs of the children in her care.

In order for a play plan to be well rounded it should include each of the different components of child development:

> *Physical   *Psychological
> *Cognitive   *Social

A good play plan will address each of these ideas on a daily basis.

Physical. Activities such as grasping (infancy,) reaching, crawling, cruising, walking, running and hopping are examples. The Nanny should include activities that make these routine developmental skills fun and exciting. New and different kinds of games may be devised to enhance the development of physical skills and coordination. Many physical activities are more appropriately engaged in outdoors. The Nanny should make a point of getting the children outdoors each day. Getting into the habit of enjoying outdoor activities will contribute to the child's good physical health. Exercise also increases a child's appetite and helps them sleep better.

Cognitive. Activities such as painting, storytelling and things as simple as talking with a child about interests and giving simple explanations are important. Many games will encourage thinking abilities, as will excursions to museums, the zoo, etc. Try simple games, such as, "How many blue things are in the kitchen?" or "Can a preschooler think categorically and learn math or colors?" Games such as this can be expanded upon to meet the cognitive needs of older children.

Psychological. Good psychological/emotional development will be enhanced by the Nanny's ability to communicate with the child and be perceptive of the child's moods and feelings, thereby encouraging the child to talk about these feelings. The atmosphere should be one where expression of feelings is allowable regardless of whether the child is happy, sad or angry. A loving Nanny who projects an attitude of care, optimism and acceptance fosters healthy psychological development.

Some activities that encourage expression include making faces (happy, sad and angry). Talk about what makes people feel happy, sad or angry and ask what makes the child feel happy, sad or angry. This encourages the child to think about and begin to understand his or her own feelings and the feelings of others. It is important to tell a child how you feel whenever it is appropriate to do so.

Another activity that will encourage expression of thoughts and feelings is asking about the child's own drawing. You can both sit down and draw pictures of yourselves and then tell each other about the picture, e.g., "This is a picture of Roger's (or Tiffany's) birthday party. He (or she) is very happy," etc. Needless to say, comments should always be age-appropriate and non-judgmental.

One of the most important contributions you can make to a child's psychological development is to increase his or her feelings of self-worth (self-esteem). The following are some important guidelines to keep in mind.

- Praise the child on a regular basis using non-evaluative, descriptive praise.
- Refrain from expecting more from the child than that for which he or she is developmentally ready, e.g., skills, behavior.
- Whenever possible ignore the negative behavior.
- Arrange opportunities for the child to succeed, to reinforce positive feelings, e.g., plan activities at which the child excels.
- Never under any circumstances resort to name-calling. Telling a child he is "bad" or "stupid," can be very damaging to a child's self-esteem.

Social. Activities that enhance a child's social development can most easily be accomplished by providing opportunities for the child to play with other children. One of the most difficult aspects of our modern age is that many Nannies and parents must make an appointment for their child to play with other children. Neighborhoods aren't what they used to be in the 1950's for instance, when most families had 3 or more children and there was always someone in the neighborhood with whom to play. The danger here is that unless the parents or Nannies understand the importance of socializing their children with age-mates, the child may not learn how to socialize well with other children until they are much older. Once they've adjusted to the group setting, they'll probably do just as well as children who have been socializing in a group for a longer period of time. However, starting school can be more traumatic than it need be if children have not been exposed to social settings with other children.

The Nanny cannot take the place of children the child's own age. Ideally, a child should have a consistent, loving Nanny and also spend several mornings each week involved in a playgroup or nursery school. This way the child can learn to interact on a one to one basis and also can learn to function as a member of a group. Nannies should make it one of their priorities either to involve the children in an established playgroup or to regularly spend time with other Nannies so that their charges will have an opportunity to interact with other children.

Playing with age-mates becomes especially appealing to the young child at about the age of 19 months. Before then, social needs can adequately be met by one-to-one relationship with Nannies and parents. In fact, the child may not be terribly interested in playing with other children before then. As the child approaches two, however, there is much more interest in other children. The age of 18 months to two years is the ideal time to plan activities that involve socialization with age-mates. This is because as children reach this age the things that kept them so happily occupied just last month perhaps, no longer hold much interest for them.

Many parents and Nannies reflect on this period of development as the time when their happy little angel underwent an enormous personality change and became a thundering bolt of lightening almost overnight. Suddenly, the child gets into everything, refuses to be diverted and can be, in general, much more difficult to care for. Some people refer to this period of development as the "terrible twos," but it doesn't have to be terrible.

The key to this stage, and as children enter other stages, is for the Nanny to adjust to the developing needs of the child and to plan activities that are more challenging and interesting. Other children fascinate children at this age. Their social skills are limited, however. They won't always share. "Mine" is a favorite word, and hitting and biting are not unusual. They'll play side by side more than they'll actually share and interact, but nevertheless they absolutely love being around each other, and as long as they're well supervised, they'll find it much more interesting than spending all their time with an adult. It's important to remember that social, civilized behavior is learned. Children at this age can begin to learn what kinds of behaviors are acceptable and which are not, but it takes another year or so before they start to consistently interact in play with other children.

The one to one relationship a child has with his or her Nanny is important in teaching the child about what kinds of behaviors are socially acceptable. Children learn behaviors by example, by imitating the adult. When a child joins a group of age-mates for the first time, however, the rules are very different. The children now learn how to assert themselves when other children treat them in an aggressive manner, or possibly they learn that aggressiveness is unacceptable. Along with learning to share, to take turns and to participate, there are many different lessons that the child may not have experienced at home. The interaction has another dimension to it since the child will not be as familiar with the other children as with his or her siblings if he or she has them.

Expect that your child may have some difficulty at first adjusting to this new set of circumstances. Getting to know other people and trying to figure out the ground rules can be stressful for some children. It's important that milestones like attending nursery school or kindergarten are taken in stride in terms of the Nanny's reaction to the child's stress since the child will pick up on any anxiety you have. What the child needs from you during this time is reassurance and positive reinforcement.

Developing A Play Plan For The Infant

Infants, especially newborns, can be more fun than you might think. Because everything is so new to them, they find excitement and wonder in almost everything we take for granted.

A play plan for an infant must be based on stimulating the five senses:

*	Sight	*	Smell
*	Sound	*	Touch
*	Taste		

Although these senses will more than likely develop well even if we don't pay special attention to stimulating them, the Nanny always does everything possible to encourage the child's optimal development and at the same time creates a special interpersonal relationship with the little person.

The typical infant play plan includes:

- Imitating animal sounds
- Reading nursery rhymes and stories
- Singing
- Dancing to music
- Massaging the skin with baby lotion

- Talking about colorful objects and what they are
- Going for a tour of the neighborhood (a walk accompanied by dialogue telling about the trees, houses and cars)
- Feeling different surfaces, e.g., hard, soft, fuzzy, scratchy, and naming each one as the baby's hand is placed on it
- Sitting in swing with baby gym attached above for the infant to explore.
- Smelling the flowers in the garden
- Practicing "pat-a-cake"
- Tasting a Popsicle and explaining "cold."—These may be made as a teething aid.
- Fruit or yogurt can be used as long as it's hard enough not to fall apart or be swallowed
- Helping the Nanny do the laundry—try putting the baby in a carrier that is similar to a backpack and take the child along while you do work around the house.

CHOOSING TOYS

Every year, millions of dollars are spent on toys. Unfortunately, children under three years of age have very little control over how those dollars are spent and they don't get to buy toys for themselves. Moreover, they are not very aware of what's available, nor are they particularly adept at communicating their preferences.

During this period of life, children are largely at the mercy of their parents when it comes to the selection and purchase of their playthings. What can you do to ensure that their toys will be appropriate and that money will be spent wisely and not wasted? There are three basic things to keep in mind.

Safety. First and foremost is safety. During the last few years, the federal government has gone a long way to protect very young children from their playthings. There are now regulations that prohibit toys manufactured for infants and toddlers from having lead-based paint, removable parts that can be swallowed or choked on, sharp edges or corners, protrusions or various other hazards. Nevertheless, it is wise to double-check all toys yourself to be sure. A good set of guidelines may be obtained from the local branch of the U.S. Consumer Product Safety Commission. The number is 1-800-638-2772. (in Maryland, the number is 1-800-492-8104). It is important to note that the Consumer Product Safety Commission is <u>not</u> able to test <u>each</u> toy coming out on the market.

Remember that many of these regulations do not apply to toys manufactured for older children, and accidents can happen when such toys find their way into the hands of an infant or toddler. For instance, small model cars are fine for an eight-year-old child who will roll the car on the floor and say "Rumm, Rumm!" However, the younger brother may say "Yumm, Yumm!" as he pops it into his mouth.

Durability. The second consideration is durability. While an older child can be instructed to take care of playthings, this is an unrealistic admonition for a child under three. Regardless of how the toy was designed to be used, infants and toddlers will chew on it, pull at it, bang it, drop it and otherwise heap abuse upon it. And they will do so with a strength that seems amazingly disproportionate to their small size! Recently, several toy manufacturers have begun to offer lifetime guarantees on some of their products. However, you would be well advised to open up all boxes and check out just how tough toys really are before you buy them.

Along these same lines, it should be noted that very young children will not only subject their playthings to physical stress, but also will expose them to dirt, grime, peanut butter and bodily fluids of all kinds. Since most objects that reach the hands of such children eventually reach their mouths too, a toy that can't be washed easily and effectively soon will become a worthless health hazard.

Play Value. The third thing to keep in mind when choosing toys for infants and toddlers is play value. That is, does the toy match the child's interests and abilities given that child's particular stage of development? While this is a very obvious question to ask, getting a straight answer sometimes can be difficult. When it comes to designing and packaging their products, some manufacturers seem to be more concerned about the adults who will select and purchase the toys than the children who will receive and play with them.

During the first three years of life, children's interests and abilities change more rapidly than during any other period in their lives, and the kinds of playthings that turn them on change quickly. Something that is too advanced and frustrating for a child at a particular stage of development may be too simple and boring for that same child within a matter of months.

As a result, the recommended age ranges that appear on toy boxes usually are greatly exaggerated and, consequently, largely inaccurate with respect to play value. It is not uncommon to see something like "for children three months to three years." Can you think of anything that will be appealing to both a three-month-old and a three-year-old?

Characteristics—Preschool and the School Age Child

	PHYSICAL	COGNITIVE	PSYCHOLOGICAL	SOCIAL
Preschool	Growth is slower. Large muscle coordination is better than small muscle or hand-eye coordination. Begins to dress self. Bones not completely calcified. Daytime nap is given up. Sleeps longer at night. High level of activity. Toilet habits established. Becomes irritable when tired, usually by end of day or after very active day.	Imitates language and behaviors. Enjoys imaginative games, fairy tales. Can speak in sentences. Play Doh, painting and coloring will hold his/her attention for longer periods of time. Wants to do more than is capable of, e.g., help with cooking, driving, etc. Interested in how things work. Asks lots of questions and has great curiosity. Doesn't know the difference between truth and untruth. Can follow simple instructions. Needs guidance.	Wants adult approval. Beginning to accept limits with less resistance. More interested in father than in earlier stages. Becoming less ritualistic. Requires the genuine interest of adults in his/her thoughts and feelings.	Begins to play cooperatively. Starts to share. Plays with members of opposite sex. Not ready for competition. Likes to have a "job" around the house. Enjoys helping. Beginning to learn what kinds of behavior are acceptable and what are not.

Characteristics—Preschool and the School Age Child

	PHYSICAL	COGNITIVE	PSYCHOLOGICAL	SOCIAL
Early School Age		Learns best when participating rather than by following abstract directions. Forgetful, but becoming more responsible. Needs adult supervision. Enjoys hobbies, collections, etc. Abilities and accuracy increasing. Beginning to understand concepts of time and money. Interest in past becoming more developed. Eager to learn, curious.	Needs adult approval. Expresses feelings. Resents being told what to do. Begins to demand own rights. Assertiveness. Great interest in friends. "Best friend becomes important. Has desire to do well. Enthusiastic.	Beginning to cooperate as a group member. Difference in interests between boys and girls becomes more apparent. More interested in activity than in end result, e.g., games, etc. Beginning to want approval of peers in addition to adults. Becoming more animated and dramatic.

Characteristics—Preschool and the School Age Child

	PHYSICAL	COGNITIVE	PSYCHOLOGICAL	SOCIAL
Middle School Years	Level of energy less than that of previous stages. Body systems near maturation. Small motor skills sharpened. Ready for handwork, e.g., model planes, crafts, etc. Growth spurts may occur, e.g., girls sometimes enter a period of rapid growth. Sleep requirement is about 10 hours. Rest period or quiet time beneficial during the day. Some children still physically immature, marked by high energy level. Posture developing.	Capable of prolonged interest. Interested in real life stories more than fairy tales. Perfectionism, wants to do well, but will become discouraged and lose interest. Argumentative over games and rules.	Has developing sense of right and wrong. Individual differences becoming distinct. More time spent in talk and discussion. Breakups of friendships occur due to difference in maturation. Likes to talk things over.	More interested in age mates of same sex. Antagonistic toward opposite sex. Cooperating more in group plans, discussions. Interested in clubs, organizations, and memberships. Develops feelings and sense of loyalty, school spirit, etc. Enjoys opportunity to express creativity through art, music, drama, etc. Dealing better with competition.

Characteristics—Preschool and the School Age Child

Characteristics—Preschool and the School Age Child	PHYSICAL	COGNITIVE	PSYCHOLOGICAL	SOCIAL
Pre-adolescence	Wide variations in maturation can begin at nine years: girls taller, heavier and about two years more mature than boys (some boys don't develop until age 17). Gangly appearance due to unevenness of growth, e.g., hand, feet disproportionate to body size. Awkwardness, poor posture not uncommon. Unstable activity level. Adult appearance developing. Eight to ten hours of sleep required.	Interested in moneymaking activities, hobbies, collections, comics, movies. Rules and fairness important. Sometimes anxious about the future.	Needs acceptance of age mates. Begins to show interest in opposite sex. Moodiness, overcritical of others and self. Self-conscious about body changes. Trying to "find himself/herself." Anxious about the future. Acts like a know-it-all, but still uncertain and unsure. Fear of ridicule by peers. Sensitive to opinions of peers and others. Seeks independence from family, but needs their moral support. Wants to make decisions.	Friends becoming more important than family. Works cooperatively in a group. Handles group responsibility well. Feelings of loyalty. Preoccupied with acceptance of group and peers. Needs guidance in understanding others, e.g., opposite sex. May respond better to teachers or adults other than parent.

CHAPTER TEN

Mothers & Babies
Common Concerns I

Assisting The Mother Of The Newborn

When we take a position helping a woman who has just had a baby, we tend to think of the position in terms of rocking and bathing a swaddled little bundle while mother is somewhere in the background resting.

Although this may occur sometimes, most mothers want to care for their infants themselves. Even in situations where a new mother says he/she wants help "caring" for the baby, the help he/she needs is usually in the form of information, i.e., "How long to breast feed", "Why is the baby crying", and support, which many times is mainly reinforcing that the baby is doing fine (and that mom is doing a good job).

Babies, especially first born, have a way of dramatically changing not only the status quo of a household but the moods and emotions of his or her parents as well. This is especially true of the baby's mother because of the physical changes her body has gone through. These changes can manifest in feelings of elation alternating with feelings of real depression. Fathers, and especially those who are involved in the care of the newborn, also experience mood swings.

They, too, need support in the form of reassurance that the atmosphere of the house will soon return to normal and the stress that everyone feels because of the change the new member has brought about, will soon disappear.

Organize The Environment

The most useful thing you can do for the new mother is organize the environment. Babies spend most of their time eating and sleeping and are awake usually no more than four to six hours a day. During this time, most mothers want to be with the baby(especially if he/she is breast feeding).

Since the latter stage of pregnancy involves a lot of spent energy in anticipation and anxiety, followed by the labor and birth which is extremely exhausting, the new mother needs rest when he/she is not caring for the baby.

Use the section of this book on Home Management to organize the home. If there are older children, refer to the Creative Play section and common concerns for sibling rivalry.

COMMON CONCERN	WHAT TO DO OR ADVISE
1. Fatigue	a. Encourage rest.
	b. Organize environment, i.e., laundry, shopping home hygiene, meals(prepare some in advance to be frozen include written instructions).
2. Depression	a. Reassure that baby is fine(discuss any concerns with nurse or pediatrician)
	b. Reassure that mother is doing great and that you can handle the house, other children, etc.
3. Breast Tenderness	a. Lanolin for nipples.
	b. Hot showers to relieve engorgement.

c. Provide a relaxed atmosphere by projecting a confident attitude. While mother is breast feeding care for the other children.

d. Advise not to use soap on nipples; soap is drying.

e. Do not wash lanolin off nipples, it won't harm the baby.

f. If nipple becomes cracked or sore, reduce time on that breast, feed only several minutes until soreness subsides.

4. Hemorrhoids

a. Advise not to strain when moving bowels.

b. Encourage foods with fiber.

c. Ask obstetrician about suppositories or creams for comfort.

CAESAREAN RECOVERY

5. Congestion (cold like symptoms)

a. Deep breathing.

b. Walking as tolerated.

6. Intestinal Gas

a. Walking as tolerated.

b. Sometimes laxatives are helpful.

c. Increase fluids.

7. Abdominal Tenderness

a. Use extra pillows for support in bed.

b. Avoid allowing older children to climb or sit on mother's lap. (Distract siblings with creative games).

COMMON CONCERNS/INFANCY

Mothers/Nannies should call the pediatrician's office any time they have questions or concerns. Pediatricians expect these calls especially from first mothers/Nannies with babies under 5 months of age.

Crying

Should you pick the baby up whenever he/she cries? Yes. Pick him up whenever possible. Babies do not become "spoiled" when they are held often. In fact, many studies have indicated that babies that are held frequently during infancy cry less later on. This is probably because they are more secure.

Comforting a crying baby

1. *FOOD*: All of a sudden an infant's hunger can seem ravenous. This perhaps is because the immature system will not send the hunger "message" to the infant's brain until the stomach has been empty for a while. You'll recognize a hunger cry. It is usually loud and repetitive. Always offer food if you suspect that the baby may be hungry. Also gastric discomfort can result from a change in diet, i.e. starting or switching formula, and if the baby is breast fed, a change in mother's diet may be the cause of baby's discomfort.

2. *BURPING*: An infant should be burped for as long as 15 minutes to help relieve gastric discomfort after eating(drinking). Be certain to burp the baby for at least that long, or until you get results. If the/she baby doesn't burp within 15 minutes, he/she probably doesn't need to, but always lie the baby on his belly after feeding, in case of regurgitation. Most babies prefer being held on your shoulder as opposed to other positions.

3. *FULFILL THE NEED TO SUCKLE*: There is nothing wrong with the use of a pacifier. Sucking is a natural instinct. Many times, the baby has had enough to eat but still feels the need to "suckle". Giving

the pacifier will fulfill the infant's suckling instinct and is helpful in soothing him.

4. *RELIEVING CONSTIPATION*: Constipation can be painful and is usually related to the baby's diet. In this situation a shrill cry of pain will be followed by sobs or gasps. If the baby is being breast fed, the chances of constipation is lessened. If there is no stool or hard stool, however, have the mother drink warm prune juice before breast feeding or offer the infant water frequently. This usually helps the breast fed baby feel more comfortable. If the baby is formula fed or has started cereal, ask the pediatrician about giving a little strained prunes from a jar and/or fruit juice. *Keep in mind babies should not be treated for constipation unless they are visually uncomfortable, i.e. straining accompanied by a hard stool, crying, etc.*

5. *RHYTHM & MOVEMENT*: Babies will often fall asleep when riding in a car or carriage probably because the motion is so similar to what they were accustomed "in utero". Bouncing gently while walking is very soothing to most babies and is likely to put even the fussiest infant to sleep. So, hold the baby firmly and put a good bounce in your walk. Baby swings are also very soothing.

6. *CHANGE OF POSITION & SCENERY*: Moving the infant from the crib to a "baby seat" adjusted at an angle, may be all he/she needs for comfort. This is true for babies up until they are able to get around on their own. Moving from the baby seat to a swing or just from tummy to lying on his side(with a rolled blanket along his back for support) is soothing.

7. *OVERTIRED BABY*: Some babies will cry when they are overtired and unfortunately trying different tactics may only be more irritating to an overtired infant. A tired cry has no pattern, but is usually low, as opposed to high pitched or loud. If you suspect that the infant is just tired, or you have tried everything you can think of, try lying the baby on his belly in his crib, reduce stimuli by drawing shades or turning off lights, offer a pacifier if you think this will be a comfort and see if the

baby will fall off to sleep. If fatigue is the problem, baby will be asleep within 15 minutes.

8. *BOWEL MOVEMENTS*: The following has been known to concern mothers/Nannies of newborns: a) constipation; b) diarrhea; or c) strange color or strange consistency of the stools. What is the "normal" stool like in a baby?

Breast-fed Babies: These babies have 2-7 bowel movements a day. These are usually very soft, liquid, absorbed into the diaper. Many times they are uneven, liquid with rough solid bits in it. In color too, anything goes—from mustard-yellow to brown to bright green. Also, these babies may not have any stools at all from one to three days. Reassure mother(and grandmother) not to worry. This is NOT constipation and nothing has to be done.

Bottle-fed Babies: These babies have 1-4 stools a day. They are harder in form and darker in color. Also, don't worry, unless baby is really pushing and uncomfortable. Call the pediatrician if a change in diet doesn't help.

9. *CONGESTION*: Everyone has mucus in their airways. By airways we mean mouth, throat, wind pipes, bronchi, and lung tissue. Mucus is constantly being produced by glands that never let the airways dry out.

We all, from time to time, cough to rid ourselves of excess mucus. However, babies do not master the technique of coughing until later. Also, while "in utero", the infant received all of her oxygen through the umbilical cord and did not use her lungs until birth. Therefore, there is a lot of leftover mucus in the airways, and as a result, newborns can be especially noisy breathers. This causes those symptoms that are similar to congestion. Do we have to do anything at all? Not necessarily. If the baby is fairly comfortable and can also drink 1 or 2 ounces without interruption, there is probably no reason to be concerned.

On the other hand, if thick mucus shows in the nostrils and baby is uncomfortable and gasping for air when drinking, then do the following:

1. Suction both nostrils. **Points of Emphasis:**

   ▪ Use a bulb syringe specifically designed for infants.
   ▪ Depress the bulb before inserting into baby's nostrils.
   ▪ Insert only 1/4 inch.
   ▪ Allow bulb to suction by releasing your thumb or fingers so it is no longer depressed.
   ▪ Remove, clean, and repeat.
   ▪ Wash bulb by suctioning clean soapy water until water runs clear, then suction clear water until fully rinsed.

NOTE: Babies do not enjoy this procedure. Be certain it is only inserted slightly so that when baby resists, his nostrils are not traumatized by the bulb syringe tip. Hold him upright as much as possible.

10. *CORD (UMBILICUS) CARE*: Within a couple of days the newborn's cord should be quite dry. If it isn't, notify the pediatrician. About 5 to 6 days after birth, the remaining tissue will be very dry. Be sure to clean around the cord at each diaper change with an alcohol prep especially if the cord was in contact with a urine soaked diaper. Report any abnormality to the pediatrician, i.e. increased redness, unusual discharge, i.e., pus and/or nasty odor. *These abnormalities may be indications of infection.* It is not uncommon for newborns to have what appears to be a *slight* brownish discharge where the dried out section of cord meets the body.

   ✓ Avoid getting the remaining tissue (cord stump) wet.
   ✓ Try to fold the diaper so that it does not get the cord wet should the diaper become saturated with urine.

11. *CARE OF THE PENIS—CIRCUMCISION*: There is some controversy regarding the need for circumcision. Many professionals claim that it is an unnecessary procedure. The practice originated as a religious ritual

for purposes of cleanliness, however, it is certainly feasible to expect that a child can be taught to keep this area of his body clean as part of this daily routine once he/she is old enough(approximately 5 years). In any case, this is the parents' decision and should be respected.

If the Baby is Not Circumcised:

The most important factor to bear in mind if the baby is not circumcised is to *leave the penis alone*, do not attempt to pull back the foreskin. This may cause the penis to bleed since in infants and toddlers the foreskin is well attached and is not designed to be pulled back. Again, a child of approximately 4-5 years old can begin to learn how to care for his personal hygiene, but check first with the pediatrician regarding care of the penis.

If the Baby is Circumcised:

- ✓ More than likely gauze will be wrapped around the tip of the penis.
- ✓ Do not try to manipulate it in any way. It will fall off by itself.
- ✓ Keep it as dry as possible. Do not immerse the baby when bathing.
- ✓ Comfort the baby if he/she suddenly becomes fussy during his first week or so.
  It could be that the urine stings the circumcised area.
- ✓ Notify the pediatrician if the penis becomes infected or bleeds more than a few drops. (See umbilicus care for signs of infection.)

12. *RASH*: Since there are a large number of different rashes, we won't attempt to list them all. We will just mention a few of the most frequent ones, and just how concerned you should be about them.

Erythema Toxicum: Babies get this between the age of 1 to 7 days. It looks like little pimples scattered over the body. Don't worry about it. Don't treat it. It will go away by it.

Newborn Acne: Yes, newborns can get acne, too from age 6 weeks to 2 years. It is hereditary. It will go away by itself.

Diaper Rash: The most common of all rashes is caused by fungi also called Monilia. Fungi like dark and wet environments. Diaper rash can occur regardless of how clean the baby is kept. Monilia is present every where, and just waits for favorable conditions to strike. Fungi can be suspected if the rash is persistent and sore. Anytime a Monilia rash is present, check the infant for thrush (see Illnesses) since the infection can travel through the baby's system and cause a rash in the diaper area. What to do? Use cotton diapers. (Disposable diapers have a plastic lining which holds moisture in). Leave the diaper area open to air for a couple of hours. Wash with lukewarm water and pat dry at each diaper change. Anytime Monilia is suspected, the pediatrician may order an ointment medication. This ointment should be used as long as the diaper rash lasts.

Other types of diaper rash are caused by:
- ✓ Diarrhea
- ✓ Teething
- ✓ Not changing the diaper often enough which can result in "ammonia dermatitis" a very painful rash that can spread to the abdomen.
- ✓ Using something to clean the diaper area that is irritating to the skin.

Heat Rash: These are bright red areas, usually on the neck or the forehead, consisting of tiny blood vessels. These are present at birth, and usually disappear by the age of 2.

Other Rashes: Some rashes are caused by bacteria, others by food allergies, etc. Some are itching, others are not. Mosquito bites are on the face and arms, and other exposed areas, when the weather is good. Flea bites are under the clothing, under the blanket, and don't depend on the season. Be sure to report all rashes and ask for advice, because the treatment that might help one type of rash, might make another worse!

13. *THUMB (FINGER) SUCKING*: There is nothing wrong with thumb sucking. There are lots of misconceptions and old "wives' tales" about the "evils" of finger sucking, as well as some horrendous ways to prevent children from sucking their fingers. This does NOT cause damage to the teeth until the permanent teeth are coming in. By this time, (age 6-7), most children give it up.

14. *VOMITING*: Almost all babies vomit or regurgitate their dinner at one time or another. Some vomit 2-3 times a day. Some just babies spit up. If the baby is doing fairly well during the rest of the day, appears satisfied, and most importantly is GAINING WEIGHT satisfactorily that is at least 4 ounces a week), we can dismiss the problem. *If the baby keeps on vomiting, looks restless, unhappy, does not gain as he/she should, that's a different matter, and we are dealing with an emergency!* In any case, keep in touch with the pediatrician. After the age of about 4 months, a sudden start of vomiting is ALWAYS a matter of concern.

15. *ENLARGED BREASTS OR GENITALS*: Some babies are born with either enlarged breasts or genitals. This is due to an increased amount of hormones in the infant's system which will subside within a week or two. Never apply ice or manipulate in any way. This is perfectly normal and will go away on its own.

16. *DISCHARGE*: Baby girls sometimes have a whitish vaginal discharge or bleeding from the vagina. This is also due to hormones and is no cause for alarm. It will go away on its own within a week or so. Vaginal discharge that develops later or in large amounts is another matter, however, and requires the pediatrician's attention.

17. *CROSSED EYES*: Crossed eyes is not abnormal as long as it is not a consistent condition. Most newborns cross their eyes intermittently and the eyes will then return to their normal position. If the infant's eyes do not resume normal position, report this to the pediatrician.

18. *HAIR LOSS*: All babies will lose most of their hair within the first two months. This is perfectly normal and is nothing to be concerned about.

19. *TREMORS OR QUIVERS*: Many infants will appear to be quivering either in isolated areas(i.e. Jaw) or will appear to be having body tremors with episodes lasting several *seconds*. This is not unusual and will eventually stop.

20. *"SOFT SPOT"*: All babies have a "soft spot" or fontanel on top of their head at birth. The fontanel enables the infant to pass through the birth canal more easily since the skull is able to compress as it passes through. This accounts for why the heads of some babies have a strange shape at birth. However, the infant's head will soon become more rounded and is no reason for concern. The soft spot will close by the time the baby reaches 18 months. You may wash this area gently without fear of hurting the baby.

21. *CRADLE CAP*: Cradle Cap is a common scalp disorder and is usually located in the area of the fontanel. It appears as crusted patches. This condition is probably due to the natural reluctance to apply pressure to that area when washing. Many hospitals send babies home with a soft scalp brush to use when shampooing. Along with the soft scalp brush, the application of oil

overnight may help loosen the crusted patches and make them easy to remove. If the area under the crusts are red and inflamed, ask the pediatrician for advice.

22. *FEEDING BLISTER*: Until your baby becomes used to the pressure of the nipple, he/she may develop a blister on her lip. This requires no treatment and will go away.

23. *COLIC:* Colic is characterized by long periods of intense crying with no apparent cause. It is most common in babies two weeks to four months of age. There is no "cure" for colic. However, a change in either the breast feeding mothers' diet (eliminating cow's milk) or the type of formula the infant is on, may help. It is important to remember the following:

- ✓ Colic will go away eventually.
- ✓ Colicky babies are in pain—which is why they are crying. Try all the comfort measures listed earlier.

- ✓ Long periods of infant crying can play havoc with *your* nerves. You must maintain your sanity by having someone else spell you for a few hours a day, otherwise it may be very difficult for you to care effectively for the baby.
- ✓ See the pediatrician to ascertain that there are no other reasons for the baby's distress.
- ✓ Give the infant as much soothing as you possibly can. *Remember, he/she is in pain.* Then after a while, place him on his belly in his crib so that both the baby and you can rest.
- ✓ If you find yourself feeling angry toward the baby, *talk to someone immediately*.
- ✓ The last thing a helpless infant in pain needs is someone either neglecting him or causing more pain.

24. *CUTTING TEETH*: Teeth are already way up in the facial bones at birth as can be seen by x-ray. However, the actual teeth cutting does not show until the age of 3 months at the earliest, and more commonly 6-9 months of age. The frontal teeth(called incisors) come in first, often starting with the lower frontals.

About 50% of all babies have a hard time, i.e. swollen and painful gums when teething. It is advisable to give the baby something hard to chew, like a plastic coated teaspoon, teething ring, and other kinds of teething items. *Refrain from anything that could be bitten off or swallowed. The pediatrician may prescribe medication for pain, if needed.*

25. *SLEEP PATTERNS*: Newborns can be expected to sleep no more than a few hours at a time, day or night, until they gain a substantial amount of weight. Low birth weight babies will take less at each feeding and subsequently will wake sooner to be fed. Breast fed babies, because of the consistency of breast milk which is thinner than formula will also need more frequent feedings because it is digested more quickly. Once the infant has reached a weight of approximately 15 pounds, he/she may sleep through the night. Prior to this, he/she/he/she will awaken at

least once and perhaps twice nightly for a feeding. Although it differs depending on the individual child, many infants begin sleeping through the night as early as 3 months. However, the average is six to eight months. Once cereal feedings begin, it would be helpful to give a cereal feeding before the parents turn in to encourage a long sleep.

Another technique is to put the infant in his room at night thus refraining from doing so during the daytime. Since the bedroom is dark and quiet, it is more conducive to an uninterrupted sleep. Routine has been known to be helpful in establishing habits and this may help if you have a port-a-crib to put the baby down in during the day. Although you should never prevent a child from sleeping, it may be helpful to provide a stimulating, active schedule for the infant during the day in order to help her make the distinction between day and night. This is especially helpful for parents of infants who are awake all night and who sleep all day.

You can expect that the newborn's sleep routine will change around 3 months of age from erratic sleep patterns to nearly sleeping through the night and taking a long morning and afternoon naps and even a late afternoon nap to awaken for a late dinner.

Just when you become accustomed to this new routine, it changes. Baby will skip one of the naps or may start awakening again in the middle of the night. Refrain from giving a bottle in the middle of the night as this may develop into a ritual. Instead, check the infant. Say "good night" as long as he/she appears well and is not in distress. Leave the room, you may have to deal with a certain amount of complaining on the infant's part, from fussing to outright yelling, but eventually baby will understand that he/she is not supposed to be a nocturnal creature. The use of a pacifier is very helpful unless there is some prejudice against it on the parents' part. It is important to remember that all infants are individual and sleep patterns will vary according to the atmosphere of the home and how you respond to your baby.

CHAPTER ELEVEN

Toddlers & Older Children
Common Concerns II

POTTY TRAINING

In the past it was not uncommon for mothers to potty train their toddlers as early as one year old. This practice was consistent with the old-fashioned theory that a child was to be controlled, for better or worse. Today, we have more information about the kinds of child-rearing practices that produce healthy children (and eventually healthy adults) and so we have let go of many of these old-fashioned ideas.

Potty training should not begin until the child shows an interest in imitating older children's or adults' use of the bathroom, or until the child shows that he is aware that he is about to urinate or move his bowels. When this will happen varies from one child to another but potty training should never be attempted during the negativistic stage of toddlerhood, when everything is "mine", "no", etc. It is not unusual for a child to still use diapers until his fourth birthday. This is nothing to worry about.

The worst thing you can do is nag the child or ridicule him in any way, i.e., "Oh babies wear diapers" or "something stinks, pee you!"

Ridicule, name calling, or teasing of this kind can be damaging to a child's self-esteem, and is absolutely never done. A child cannot distinguish between himself and his excrement as being separate, therefore, when someone elaborates on how horrible a diaper smells, the child will interpret that as meaning that he, the individual, smells. Therefore, it is best to relax regarding toilet habits and to let nature take its course.

The better preschools now accept children who are not yet potty trained because they understand the significance of not applying pressure. All children learn to use the potty usually by the age of four or so, and, depending upon the child, introduction of the potty could begin as young as two. Children learn most effectively under the following circumstances:

- When cared for by knowledgeable, relaxed adults who do not nag or try to control.
- When in an atmosphere of convenience, i.e., outside in the summer, where big-boy/girl (training) pants can be worn without fear of 'accidents' damaging rugs or furniture.
- When exposed to older children whom they will imitate.
- When cared for by adults who praise the positive behavior and ignore the negative or 'accidents'.
- When a routine, structure for learning is in place, i.e., once the child has given some indication of being ready, putting the child in training pants at a certain time each day until you are successful *as long as there is no resistance.*
- When a child resists, the adults drop the subject, put diapers on without comment, and try again later (i.e., several weeks later).

The Potty Training Outline

As your child approaches her second birthday, observe her for any interest on her part regarding potty training, i.e., interest or attempts to imitate older children's bathroom habits, or her letting you know when she's urinating or moving her bowels. (Some children even ask to have their diapers changed!)

❖ Put a potty chair bathroom near the toilet.
❖ Ask your child if he'd like to try sitting on his new chair (with diapers and pants on for the first few times).
❖ For the first week of potty training, set aside one hour on three different days to spend in the kitchen (or any other uncarpeted room) to begin practicing the use of the potty chair.
❖ Choose some books or games that she enjoys most.
❖ Offer plenty of fluids prior to beginning.
❖ Enthusiastically talk about 'trying out' the potty chair, remove the diaper, and ask your child to try sitting on it. (It may feel cold to her since she's not used to sitting on a rim, and she may be uncomfortable at first so don't be disappointed if she's not thrilled about it.) Tell her you'll read her a great story while she sits on the potty chair and tries to use it.
❖ Offer some more fluids once she is seated on the chair. If she refuses to sit on the chair, that's okay; let her walk around and ask her again in ten minutes or so.
❖ The main objective at this point is to introduce the idea to your child. Don't expect success the first time. Right now, you just want to get her used to sitting on it; don't nag.
❖ If she uses the potty, praise her enthusiastically! If she doesn't, that's fine too.
❖ At the end of the hour, put her diaper back on. Do not alter the schedule by making it either longer or shorter. If your child uses the floor instead of the chair, nonchalantly clean it up. Comments such as "Oops, we missed" are best. Never make your child feel ashamed or embarrassed by either your attitude or comments. This will hinder the process. (Some children have been known to become constipated for

weeks during the process of potty training because of the stress they felt; therefore, we always maintain a very relaxed attitude!)

❖ During the second week, increase the time from one hour to two. *Unless your child is resisting*, following the same procedure as during the first week.

❖ If your child resists and does not want to use the potty, put his diaper back on and refrain from talking about it. Drop the entire matter for several more weeks or longer until you feel he may be ready.

❖ Normal potty training involves success along with intermittent 'accidents'. Be careful not to show either disgust or disappointment in the event your child forgets or is uncooperative.

❖ During the third week, you may increase either the time intervals or the number of days that week depending upon how well your child is doing. Remember, a relaxed attitude is best.

❖ For the first three weeks, be sure to maintain a potty-training schedule, beginning and finishing at predetermined times; otherwise, you may be setting yourself and your child up for disappointment.

❖ Keep your child in diapers during naps, at bedtime, and on any long outings for the first few months that he is trained.

❖ After two months or longer, limit excess fluids before nap time and begin putting your child down for a nap without a diaper. Continue, depending on the outcome.

❖ Follow the above procedure at night after your child is able to get through nap time for a month or longer without wetting the bed.

❖ All children have 'accidents', especially when they are feeling stressed, unhappy, or uncomfortable; expect this, and respond nonchalantly.

❖ Be sure to remind your child about using the bathroom before going out, after meals, before bedtime, etc.

❖ Do not set a date by which you want your child to be trained. Potty training should never be a contest between your child and another child you know. Your relaxed attitude towards the whole process is the key to success.

TEMPER TANTRUMS

All toddlers from time to time will express their frustration and anger in the form of a tantrum. It is not unusual, nor does it mean that the child is "spoiled", "incorrigible", or any other name that might come to mind when we think of temper tantrums.

The frustration and anger that the toddler/preschooler feels is based partly on:

- Their urge (i.e., everyone else's urging) to be a "big boy/girl", use the potty, etc. and in general, a preoccupation with being "big" is conflicting with all of the things they are still not able to do (i.e., use the stove, go outside alone, etc). Therefore, they are experiencing a constant "push/pull" regarding what they want to do and what they are truly capable of doing.

  This is confusing and frustrating to a youngster in this stage of development. She's constantly getting double messages—"act like a big girl" alternating with "don't touch that, that's not for little girls", etc.

  The toddler has a strong desire to express his independence, his selfhood. He has watched others command the environment and he now wants his turn. His verbal skills are improving every day and he's learning the power of language, but still unable to articulate his opinions, ideas and feelings.

The frustration that occurs with the many limitations toddlers feel will eventually accumulate and become anger. This is the point when the tantrum takes over. Although the developmental forces behind the tantrums are perfectly normal and healthy, it is difficult to deal with a child who strikes or acts out at others in anger. It takes experience before the toddler understands the implications of his angry action, i.e. hitting with objects, throwing things, etc.

Keep in mind that part of this behavior is the result of the toddler's *limited impulse control.* Wants, needs, emotions, etc. are automatic and not usually within his/her control. This may be a difficult concept for many parents/Child Care Professionals to grasp, especially if they are convinced that their child is particularly bright. Keep in mind, however, the immense need to scream and pound the floor is overpowering to a child of this age and *should be released, as long as the child doesn't hurt himself or anyone else in the process.*

Self-control is not an attribute that toddlers are well known for and it will be a disappointed parent/Child Care Professional who tries to insist on self-control at this age. Probably the best thing we can do is practice self control ourselves and teach by example. *Tantrums should be ignored* unless the child is hurting himself, someone else, or destroying something valuable. Like many other behaviors, the more attention we give it, even negative attention, the greater likelihood the child will repeat the behavior. *Also, children should be allowed to express their anger.* Anger is a normal response to frustration, etc. Expressing it is healthy. There is no need to be embarrassed if a child in your charge throws a major tantrum in public either. If people look at you with disrespect because your child is so ill mannered, ignore them too. Obviously they don't know a lot about child development.

Children have been known to throw tantrums in public because they have come to learn that their mother/Child Care Professional will react strongly, sometimes be giving in, just to quiet them. This is a mistake. There will be occasions when you will have to change your plans, i.e., leave church if your child is screaming at the top of his lungs, etc., but unless it is absolutely necessary, hold your ground and don't give in. *Your consistent calm affect in the face of a tantrum is the most effective tool you have,* and remember, if you lose your temper in response to a major tantrum, you are reinforcing that a loss of control is acceptable behavior.

SETTING LIMITS (DISCIPLINE)

There are several ways to avoid tantrums. Probably the most useful idea is to understand the dynamics of development at this stage. There is a need to explore and try new things. The toddler needs to feel that he is in control of some aspects of his life.

The "terrible twos" is the same stage where tantrums are most prevalent. This stage of development got its name from the toddlers need to "get into" everything and react to limits with a tantrum. A good way to circumvent difficult situations is to *organize the environment* to minimize the number of times you'll have to say, "don't touch that". (It is important to refrain from overusing the word "no"). Childproofing the home is the way to this (see Home Management).

Another effective method is to plan the child's time so that he is not idle. This does not mean you have to play with him constantly, but that you will provide enough of a stimulating environment and atmosphere using acceptable stimuli (and materials) so that the child is not left to his own devices (see Creative Play).

Toddlers are curious, inquisitive, and in absolute awe of so much of what we take for granted. It has been said that toddler hood is the best time to introduce a second language, a musical instrument and other skills because a child of this age has the mind of a sponge. He is soaking up information constantly and enjoying every minute of it (until limits are placed on her).

You need to encourage this inquisitiveness by providing a safe, stimulating environment, which challenges the child with acceptable age-appropriate materials. *This curiosity and thirst for knowledge should be fostered.* It should never be dampened by a negative, overly controlling authority figure, who is always saying "no", but instead with an enthusiastic, adventuresome role model who will be as positive as possible and set consistent limits of behavior that is unacceptable.

One of the best methods to use when you need to set limits is *diversion*. Diffusing the situation with comments like, "Oh, look at this", or "Wow, do I have a great surprise for you", said with *a lot* of enthusiasm can effectively divert the toddler's attention to a more productive pastime. It should be noted, however, that most children will soon catch on to this commonly used technique before long and may go through a stubborn stage of refusing to be distracted. One very inventive Child Care Professional got around this behavior by planning ahead and "stashing" a number of intriguing "surprises" that the child had not seen before. This worked very well. (Be sure that all surprises are safe and never use food or candy as a surprise).

Another form of diversion is a special game or any other activity that a child particularly enjoys. This may not always be possible though because of time restraints, so a surprise "stash" can come in handy. It is wise to keep certain toys up, out of reach to be used only at certain times. Rotating toys is a common practice used by the Child Care Professional and is discussed more in the Creative Play Chapter.

Always avoid confrontation and/or power struggles. A toddlers need to feel some sense of control is a normal part of her healthy development. We don't want to reinforce her sense of powerlessness by asserting out control just for the sake of proving who's "boss". There are many ways to make a child feel secure other than involving ourselves in power struggles. It is far better to use diversion for the sake of maintaining a loving environment not to mention the significance of maintaining the child's developing sense of self-esteem. The only exception would be if the child were in danger or potentially in danger of hurting himself, someone else or something valuable.

There is no need to worry about "teaching the child that he cannot have everything he wants". Doubtless we have all heard someone say that, however, there will be plenty of opportunities for the child to learn that he can't have everything he wants without us going out of our way to prove it to him.

Other than organizing the environment and using diversionary techniques, another important factor to use to reduce the amount of times you will have to set limits is consistency. In order for a Child Care Professional to be consistent, she needs to possess a certain amount of self-discipline. It's sometimes inconvenient to follow through after we've said, "Ricky, if you don't stop pulling the cat's tail, you'll have to leave the room", especially if we are busy with another child, etc. However, it is vital that we do indeed follow through if the child repeats the behavior after being told the consequences. Otherwise, we are letting the child know that our word cannot be trusted. Consequently, the child will not respond to our future requests, resulting in more and more incidents of unpleasantness.

Inconsistency also results in the formation of negative Child Care Professional/child behavior patterns. Once you get into the habit of not following through (resulting in the child being punished, resulting in a less that pleasurable atmosphere for everyone, resulting in an unhappy child and Chief Care Provider), it is hard to change the pattern to one that is healthy and positive. The adult is responsible for maintaining a healthy atmosphere and needs to be consistent so that the child knows what the limits are.

A common tactic you should avoid is that of making nonsensical or unlikely threats that you would never follow through on even if you were a master of *self*-discipline and consistency. For example, "If you do that again, I'll put you in your room for a *week*!", or "Stop that or I'll knock your head off", or "I'll have an absolute fit if you do that one more time". Using these kinds of nonsensical tactics that could never possibly be realized will only result in the child understanding that you *won't* follow through with what you say you will do. It can also teach the child that losing patience and making threats is an acceptable way to behave.

Guilt tactics are also taboo, i.e., "Wait until Mom finds out what you did. She'll be so sad", or, "I can't believe that a big boy like you could do such a terrible thing". This could damage a child's self esteem and is not a useful way to set limits, even if our own mothers used this tactic.

One of the more acceptable consequences to employ when a child acts our or misbehaves is to make him leave the room. Isolating the child from other people, briefly (approximately 3-7 minutes depending on the age of the child), tells the child that other people do not want to be around or be a part of behavior they find socially unacceptable. It is in a true sense a form of ostracizing the child, letting him know that others don't want to be around the behavior he displayed. In preschools, it is referred to as a "time out" and it may possibly be in conflict with the philosophy of "condemning the behavior and not the child". Unfortunately, it is not possible to apply consequences to the behavior without applying them to the child as well. We can't make the behavior leave the room, while the child continues to play uninterrupted. Discuss this method of limit setting with the children's parents in order to be certain that they are in agreement. It is possible they may have more methods that are more effective with their children that have not been included here.

The manner and affect we assume when using limit-setting techniques is significant also. It is important to remain calm, don't allow the child to control *your* behavior (you are supposed to be influencing him). If the child screams, kicks and pounds the floor after being taken from the room, let him get the anger out, don't react unless he is damaging something, hurting himself or someone else.

Gradually, what should happen with calm consistent limit setting is that the child will learn *at her own pace and begin* to control her impulses and behavior, because she understands that *you can be counted on* to follow through with setting limits? Children learn through the example of others to respect to rights of other people. But they must be developmentally ready to control their impulses and delay immediate gratification. This is a difficult task for the toddler who has a limited ability to grasp the meaning of "later" or "tomorrow".

This is learned more readily, however, when the adult makes the consequences of negative behavior, i.e., "I will make you leave the room if you throw anymore of your food", and then follows through the *first time* the child repeats the negative behavior after she has been told the consequences. Responding the first time will also alleviate the possibility of you getting more angry. Tactics such as counting to three, i.e., "By the time I count to three, you had better move away from there", Is merely making a game out of a responsibility that should be dealt with more efficiently.

Any time you must set limits, it should be done:
   Directly, i.e., immediately without procrastination;
   Honestly—present *realistic* consequences;
   Calmly—without losing your temper;
   Swiftly—implement consequences right away. No counting to three or giving second chances;
   Tenaciously—insist that the child actually leave the room and stay out of the room for the appropriate amount of time (3-7 minutes, shorter times apply to younger children), plus you may have to keep returning the child to the other room; and
   Objectively—try not to personalize the behavior and become angry with the child, after the child comes back into the room, don't talk about the incident, forget it. Be as loving and kind as you usually are, the incident is over.

OBSTACLES TO LIMIT SETTING

Guilt is a common obstacle to maintaining consistent limits. If you feel unable to follow through you need to evaluate the quality of the care and interaction you are providing. If you spend little time playing, talking, etc., perhaps you need to re-evaluate the time you spend with the child (See Creative Play). If you are spending valuable time with the child, it could be a lack of self-discipline on your part that keeps you from being consistent.

A lack of self-discipline usually shows up in other ways other than the inability to set limits. It will probably show in your schedule or rather lack of a consistent schedule. It helps to write down all of your duties and organize your time (see Child Care Professional Process). Some Do's and Don'ts for setting limits:

➤ **DO**
  - ➤ Ignore negative behavior as much as possible—divert
  - ➤ Praise the "good" behavior consistently and enthusiastically
  - ➤ Provide opportunities for the child to feel "in control" (i.e., would you like to go for a walk or ready a story?).
  - ➤ Childproof environment—remove anything that is within reach that you don't want handled
  - ➤ Devise an interesting "play pen" (see Creative Play)
  - ➤ Say, "Please don't do that" instead of "no".
  - ➤ Use diversion as a limit setting technique
  - ➤ "Stash" some surprises for difficult times
  - ➤ Respond to the behavior *immediately*—never wait, or bring it up after it has occurred
  - ➤ Encourage inquisitiveness, foster curiosity
  - ➤ Rotate toys
  - ➤ Avoid confrontations and power struggles
  - ➤ Maintain consistency
  - ➤ Follow through with consequence immediately
  - ➤ Consult with parents regarding limit-setting techniques
  - ➤ Remain calm
  - ➤ Display an example you would want the child to mimic under stress
  - ➤ Present consequences honestly
  - ➤ Remain tenacious regardless of how many times you have to make the child leave the room, etc.
  - ➤ Remain objective and don't take the behavior personally, the child is exerting her independence, not deliberately annoying you

➤ DON'T

- ➤ Use consequence with children too young to conceptualize them (15 months and younger)—*use diversion only*
- ➤ Call names, i.e., bad boy/girl, nasty, baby, etc. This is damaging to a child's developing sense of confidence and self esteem
- ➤ Leave things around that you don't want handled by the child—childproof!!
- ➤ Say "no" or "no-no". Firmly say, "Please don't do that" or "I don't like that"
- ➤ Spend idle time—go for a walk, listen to (and talk about) music, read stories
- ➤ Attempt to control a child's behavior with negatives, use positive diversionary techniques
- ➤ Prevent the child from displaying anger or frustration
- ➤ Use food or candy as a "surprise" or a "reward" for good deeds
- ➤ Involve yourself in confrontations—divert
- ➤ Reinforce a toddler's sense of powerlessness by asserting control unnecessarily
- ➤ Expect others, i.e., parents to be as consistent as you are
- ➤ Use unrealistic consequences, i.e., "You'll stay in your roof for a week", or ones that are obviously nonsense
- ➤ Withhold food (bed before dinner) as a consequence
- ➤ Hit, strike, spank or otherwise physically hurt a child as a consequence (hitting only serves to vent your anger, teaches physical violence as a reaction to stress and also teaches that losing control when angry is acceptable
- ➤ Use "going to bed" as a consequence. It could result in making the young child think sleeping is a punishment
- ➤ Create negative patterns of behavior to begin with
- ➤ Use guilt tactics or talk about the misbehavior after it is over
- ➤ Employ new or different limit setting techniques without first discussing them with the parent(s)

> ➤ Allow the child to control your behavior
> ➤ Expect more "impulse control" than a child is capable of
> ➤ Expect the child to learn control without good examples being set

BE REALISTIC IN YOUR GOALS FOR GOOD BEHAVIOR

Regardless of how consistent you are, how perfect an example you set, or how much time you spend childproofing, devising a play plan, or anything else, every child, if he/she is growing an developing normally will have tantrums, act out and, in general, be somewhat difficult at times to be around. Expect this, and don't be disappointed or feel like you've failed somehow. There is no such thing as a perfectly behaved child all of the time. Anyone with such an expectation will be disappointed. Expect that there will be times when the child may be persistent and stubborn, loud or actually embarrassing because of her behavior. This is no reflection on your child rearing techniques, but simply the emergence of a personality that is as multifaceted as your own. The difference being that we are old enough and wise enough to know what is socially acceptable. The toddler doesn't. But as certain as he or she is to challenge your patience, there will be as many or more times when his charm and sweetness is irresistible.

SIBLING RIVALRY

There has been much said and written about sibling rivalry and how much time should elapse between the first born and the birth of a second child. There are many theories, but perhaps one of the most important things to remember is, sibling rivalry is not a condition isolated within the time period immediately following the birth of a second or third child. It is a condition which presents itself regardless of how far apart children are spaced, how many children there are in a given family and regardless of the ages of the children. However, the *degree* of sibling rivalry when siblings are closely spaced is substantially increased when there is less than three years between them.

In general, in homes where children are spaced three or more years apart, the atmosphere is much more pleasant and conducive to good care practices than in homes where the spacing is less than three years. In the latter cases, harsh feelings and even physical violence between siblings is common.

The difficulties between closely spaced siblings are easy to understand if you consider the normal course of social development. If a one-year old child is confronted with a newborn sibling, he does not immediately feel threatened. He is still very much concerned with his initial explorations of the home. Therefore, the sibling—who spends much of the day sleeping in the crib—does not constitute much of an intrusion. Six to eight months later, however, this situation changes dramatically. Now the older child's primary focus is on establishing a relationship with the key people in his life—his primary caregivers. At the same time, the younger child has begun to crawl, and because she now can get into a lot more trouble, she requires a great deal of attention from caregivers. That attention usually comes at the expense of the older child. Since attention equals love in his mind, intense jealousy is the natural result.

In fact, expressions of dislike for the younger child at this point are healthy signs. They indicate the older child has been receiving a lot of affectionate attention and, indeed, has "something to lose". But when he expresses such feelings in the only way he knows how, his caregivers—the very people whose affectionate attention he is desperately trying to win back, often castigate him. This compounds the problem and confuses the olds child even more. Under such circumstances, many delightful, happy-go-lucky one-year olds turn into rather sad and surly two-year olds as their once rosy outlook on the world gradually sours.

Meanwhile, unlike the other child—who at least spent the first year-and-a half or so of life in a very warm and accepting environment, the younger child is exposed to feelings of hostility and is, in some cases, routinely subjected to physical abuse from very early on. The younger child quickly learns defensive tactics, such as crying before being hit, and eventually she learns how to retaliate as well. Now the Child Care Professional and parents are not only faced with the problem of breaking up fights between the children, they can't even tell who started it. And you can imagine what happens to this already unpleasant picture if a third child is added to the scene at this stage of the game.

Life is very different when the spacing between siblings is three years or more. Under these circumstances, by the time the younger child has begun to crawl, the older child has firmly established his relationship with his caregivers and he has securely staked out his position in the home. He is now moving on to the other interests, spending a lot of time with other people, especially age mates and becoming involved in many more activities outside of the home. Of course, there are still moments when things are not perfect between the siblings, but for the most part, intense feelings of jealousy and hostility are less likely than feelings of acceptance and even affection. This makes life much easier and nicer for both the children and the Child Care Professional.

COPING WITH CLOSELY SPACED SIBLINGS

If you find yourself in a situation with closely spaced siblings, try to remember the social dynamics involved and act accordingly. Do not allow the older child to abuse the younger one, but keep in mind that his harsh feelings are normal. Also, it is important to realize that attention equals love to a young child, and he will not be able to understand or accept lengthy explanations about how family members should get along. The only thing that will make him feel better are regular sessions of undivided attention from the adults he cares about (and that does not mean reading him a story while the sibling is sleeping on your lap). Finally, try to avoid making a big fuss over the baby right in front of him. He's got a lot to lose and his capacity to deal with the situation is limited, so make every effort to keep from rubbing his nose in it. Other helpful suggestions include:

Talk about the older child in positive terms when he can overhear you, i.e., "Isn't Ricky a great little guy? He's so big, etc. etc". Do this at least twice a day.

When you are busy with the older child and baby begins to fuss, instead of going to the baby immediately, say to the baby, "Just a minute Kenny, I'm busy with Ricky right now".

Reinforce with the older child how much more he can do compared with the baby, i.e., "Your such a big boy. You can come with me to the store, but the baby has to stay home".

Encourage the older child to help with the baby whenever possible, as long as he is willing. Don't force or nag.

Consistently reinforce the advantages of being the "big brother/sister", i.e., "Pretty soon you'll be able to teach the baby to walk and talk".

To avoid sibling rivalry in families with older children, in addition to the above tactics, these basic guidelines apply:

Never compare one child's progress with another's

Be aware of the distribution of your time and attention among the siblings

Whenever appropriate, rules should apply to all children without exception

PART THREE

Home Health Care Skills

CHAPTER TWELVE

Nutrition

FOOD AND OUR PHYSICAL & EMOTIONAL HEALTH

Everyone knows the significance of food for physical health and well-being. However, most people do not apply this to their day-to-day habits. There is little doubt that we have all heard how important it is to eat a balanced diet, but since we do not see the immediate results of eating or not eating a balanced diet, most people ignore what they have heard countless times about the significance of that balance. On the physical level, history has told us about the development of scurvy in sailors who were without vitamin C on long ocean trips. We know that without protein, wounds cannot heal. Studies have shown how the "pectin" found in apples may reduce cholesterol levels in the human body when eaten after a meal high in fats and cholesterol, thus reducing the chances of heart disease. Research is presently being conducted in areas of food combining and the effect one experiences on the human energy levels after the intake of large amounts of sugar and/or caffeine. Because all of these types of physical changes cannot be "seen" immediately, most people do not practice good eating habits, and consequently are less healthy. As a Nanny you should be educated about the significance of a balanced diet.

In addition to the effect of our diet on our physical well-being, the food we eat plays an important role in our emotional health. The B vitamins, for instance have been proven to be helpful in relieving stress. They have also been helpful in relieving PMS.

Low Fat Eating

As good as it is that many people are choosing to eat more healthy, it should be kept in mind that a child's nutritional needs differ from that of an adult. It is essential that the child's diet contain enough calories and nutrients to ensure proper growth and development. Diets which are too low in fat can compromise development up until adolescence and until the child has attained his or her full height. Therefore, if the majority of the child's main meals are low in fat, be sure that when choosing snacks, foods higher in fat are chosen. Cheese, whole milk, peanut butter and ice cream as snacks for the child that lives in a "low fat household" will ensure that the child's needs are being met. Always avoid food that adds fat without adding nutrients, such as French fries and other fried or greasy foods. Bear in mind that meats are one of the highest sources of fat in our diets; therefore, if your child is a meat-eater, supplementing snack-time with high fat foods may not be necessary.

Sugar

Recent studies show that sugar does NOT cause a child to be "hyper". It is more likely that this association is made when adults watch children get more and more excited at birthday parties after consuming large amounts of sugar-laden soda, cake and candy. The "hyper" behavior we see under these circumstances probably has more to do with the excitement over whatever is going on rather than the sugar.

Nevertheless, the amount of sugar your child ingests should be kept to a minimum. Many people have a natural "sweet tooth" and most of us enjoy food high in sugar content. Unfortunately, the nutrient value in high sugar foods is usually low. In households where large amounts of sweets are available, children tend to develop the habit of eating these foods, and then have a hard time eating healthy foods. Always keep in mind that the habits you teach now will have a significant impact on the child's future health.

Vitamins

If a child will not eat well, or if a child avoids particular food group completely, supplements should be considered. Multivitamins have been used almost exclusively. However, care should be taken that the child is not receiving more than the recommended amount of certain vitamins. In excess, vitamins that are non-water soluble can be harmful.

One creative way to get nutrients into your children is to purchase a "Juicer" It is a machine that grinds fruits and vegetables into liquid. The juice of raw fruits and some vegetable can be added to fruit juice, or used with fruit juice to make frozen treats that actually taste very sweet. Juices from the juicer can be also be used in gravies, or any recipe that requires a liquid. Whatever you choose, the Juicer is a wonderful way to be sure that your children get the vitamins and minerals they need.

Iron

Don't give iron unless prescribed by the doctor.

Fluoride

In towns where the water does not contain fluoride, children should take fluoride in order to have good tooth development. Discuss this with the child's dentist, and be certain to find out for your employers information both advantages and disadvantages of taking fluoride so an informed decision can be made. Keep in mind that one dentist or pediatrician may have one opinion while another dentist and/or pediatrician may have another. Never accept medical or dental advice without questioning it. Get the facts and discuss them with your employer.

Salt, Sugar, Condiments

Avoid adding anything to the child's food. It is usually unnecessary and, since many people are in the habit of adding these things before they have even tasted their food, it can be habit forming. Remember that the child will mimic your actions, so you too, must refrain from adding these things to your meal in the child's presence. As difficult as this may be for you, keep in mind for your own health that these items are nutritionally useless and may contribute to health problems later. Sugar is especially harmful to the developing teeth of children.

Fresh Fruits And Raw Vegetables

Fresh fruits and raw vegetables should be on hand in every home and offered routinely as snacks. Fresh fruits are naturally sweet and contain all the sugar anyone could need. Many Nannies have been amazed at how eagerly children will eat raw vegetables, e.g., carrots, celery and even peeled potatoes. Even if they are in the habit of eating empty calories (junk foods,) you can still restrict the junk food and elaborate on how delicious the fresh fruit is. Creating these kinds of nutritional habits can result in a longer, healthier life for the children in your care and is one of the best habits you can teach them.

Liquids

Offer liquids frequently in the form of water, juices or milk, especially in hot weather. Do not give soft drinks; they can damage the teeth. Try to encourage both the babies and older children in your charge to drink water. You could investigate the possibility of renting a water cooler for the home. They are not expensive and the water may taste better than what comes out of the tap. Also, inexpensive home water filters make drinking water more enjoyable.

THE VEGETARIAN

Children who grow up as vegetarians can remain healthy and fit throughout their lives. That is because some meats contain large amounts of fat as well as a variety of chemicals. The chemicals found in meats range from the antibiotics that are fed to cows to keep them healthy to processes that sanitize the meat. Many people who are not strict vegetarians have cut down on their intake of meat, especially red meat, if not for any other reason than they prefer a diet lower in fat, easy on the stomach and more economical. It is a fact that there is much more protein available from vegetable and grain sources than from meat.

In order to get enough protein in the vegetarian diet, combine beans and grains in equal amounts, or combine beans and a lesser quantity of dairy, or grains and a lesser quantity of dairy. Any one of these three preceding food combinations will provide adequate protein. Using tofu and other soy products is another popular way to add protein to the diet.

Dr. Arlene Spark, associate professor of nutrition at New York Medical College, has developed a food pyramid for vegetarians. Dr. Spark advises that vegetarians should consume 3-5 teaspoonfuls of vegetable oil, one tablespoonful of Blackstrap molasses and one tablespoonful of Brewers yeast daily to round out their nutritional needs. These extras are needed for those who eat no animal products at all, as well as those who consume eggs and dairy products as part of their usual food intake. Please consult your doctor if you plan any kind of total vegetarian diet.

VITAMIN/MINERAL CHART

Vitamin A	Liver, yellow fruit, butter, margarine, whole milk, cheese, cream, green and yellow vegetables	Body growth, health of eyes, health of skin
Vitamin B	Wheat germ, lean pork, yeast, liver and other organ meats, cereals and grains	Nerve function, healthy appetite
Vitamin C	Citrus fruits, peppers, melons, berries, tomatoes, broccoli	Strength of blood vessels, health of teeth and gums, healing of wounds
Vitamin D	Liver, eggs, fish oil, milk, sunshine	Building and maintenance of bones and teeth
Vitamin E	Dark green, leafy vegetables, nuts, vegetable oils	Function of red blood cells
Vitamin K	Spinach, kale, cabbage, cauliflower, pork liver	The clotting of blood
Protein	Meat, eggs, nuts, beans	Tissue growth, healing of wounds
Potassium	Bananas, apricots, strawberries, oranges and orange juice, chicken, beef, cherries, dates, figs	Maintaining healthy body chemistry, organ function
Calcium	Turnip greens, kale, sardines, milk, cheese, cottage cheese, yogurt, buttermilk	Growth and repair of bones and teeth

Source: Massachusetts General Hospital Diet Manual

FOOD PYRAMID

In 1989, the USDA assembled a committee of independent nutritionists to develop new national dietary guidelines and a visual way to represent them. The committee established the Food Pyramid with six categories instead of the old "basic four." In addition, a chart was developed indicating recommended servings per category.

The food pyramid visually represents which foods should be eaten on a daily basis in proportion to others. The most recent pyramid indicates that the bread/grain group is the category from which we should eat the most—six to eleven servings per day. The next is vegetables at 5 servings and fruits at 4 servings per day. The next category is the milk/dairy group at two servings daily (double that for children, teenagers and pregnant women,) and the meat/fish group at two servings daily. Fats, oils and sweets are also included in the pyramid. It is suggested that they be used sparingly. It is important to keep in mind, however that there is debate in the medical community regarding the current Food Pyramid. Critics have said that since this recent Pyramid was published, the population has become more obese. Some nutritionists say that the increase in obesity in our country is not associated with the Food Pyramid. However, it is expected that it will undergo some revisions in the near future.

Today, more Americans than ever are obese. This is ironic considering that never before has there been more information in the media or more emphasis on nutrition and the role it plays in disease prevention. Diet alone has been linked to cancer, diabetes, heart disease, hypertension, stroke, osteoporosis and, of course, obesity. According to the U.S. Department of Health and Human Services "35% of all cancer deaths may be related to what we eat," and Harvard Medical School, in an April 1993 press release (Associated Press) said "You may lower your risk of stroke up to 68% by eating five servings of fruits and vegetables daily." Obesity afflicts one in three adults and one in four children in the United States.

Therefore, it is indisputable that diet plays a major role in good health and disease prevention.

For more information on the Food Guide Pyramid write to USDA Consumer Information Center, Pueblo, CO 81009. Specify document #116G (as of March 2000) and include a check for $1 made out to The Superintendent of Documents. Please call 719-948-4000 to verify the document number as it is updated regularly throughout the year.

Infant Feeding

By the time you begin caring for any infant, the decision has been made by the mother whether to breast-feed or bottle feed. Breast-feeding is, of course, being done by the mother and is best for the baby because breast milk is easier for the baby to digest and contains all the right nutrients in the right amounts. Breast milk also contains antibodies that boost the baby's immunity against illnesses. Keep in mind however, it is possible that breast milk can be given to the baby in a bottle by someone other than the baby's mother once it has been "expressed" (mechanically removed from the breast, via a pump or by hand). This allows the mother to be away for a period of time or sleep through the night while you or the baby's father take care of the night feedings.

In either case, it's important to know that 90% of babies are NOT hungry for the first 2-3 days after birth. Rather, they are sleepy. You can offer them food, but don't be concerned if the baby is somewhat disinterested at first.

When To Offer The Bottle Or Breast

Babies should be fed "on demand" as opposed to being fed on a set schedule. The phrase "demand feedings" should not be taken too literally. Don't wait for baby to bellow with ravenous hunger before offering food. Anticipate the baby's needs. After the first 2-3 days, expect that a normal size infant (approximately 6 pounds at birth for females, 7 for males) will be hungry about every 2-3 hours around the clock for the first month or two. Don't let a pattern develop where the baby has to be ravenous before he or she is fed.

It is not necessary to wake the baby up to feed him or her as it is never a good idea to wake a sleeping baby unless absolutely necessary. Instead, have everything ready so that upon waking, the baby can be fed promptly.

A week old baby of any weight should drink approximately 1 to 1 1/2 oz. at a time, but if he or she drinks less, that's all right, too. Of course, as the baby gets older, he will take up to 4 ounces at a time and about 20 ounces or more per day. Please keep in mind that these figures should not be taken literally as there are many individual variations in feeding habits depending on the size of the baby. The one factor to keep in mind is, "Is the baby gaining weight?"

Weight gain is the major barometer in determining how well nourished the infant is. The only exception being that all babies lose a pound or two during the first few days following birth. This is due to the fact that baby is not being nourished constantly as when in the uterus. Weight loss during the first few days is perfectly normal, however, the baby should develop an appetite during the end of the first week of birth and begin gaining it right back.

In early infancy, if the baby falls asleep in your arms while feeding, allow feeding to continue as long as the baby wants. Many times, the baby will continue sucking vigorously even when sound asleep, but will soon let go. Never put a child to bed with a bottle.

Burping

Help the baby burp right after feeding. This is a must, especially with bottle-fed babies due to the air bubbles that are present in the formula. Air bubbles cause a lot of discomfort and cramps, and the baby who has not been burped properly is unable to get those air bubbles up without help. Hold the baby upright over your shoulder and pat the back gently. The baby will usually burp within an average of 8 to 15 minutes. Breast-fed babies may not need to burp as much as bottle-fed. However, as the baby's appetite increases and he or she consumes more, it is a good idea to encourage the baby to burp midway through the feeling as well as when finished.

BEGINNING SOLID FOODS

Some babies are perfectly content and thriving on breast milk or formula and nothing else for the first 3-5 months of their life. If you notice that formula or the breast milk alone does not satisfy (crying unrelieved by other comfort measures, or suddenly drinking large volumes of formula) talk to the pediatrician about beginning solid food. Usually two teaspoons of cereal to one tablespoon of formula mixed well is a good way to start.

Ask the pediatrician which type of cereal should come first. Rice is commonly given, however, oatmeal cereal is believed to be easier to digest and is less constipating.

THE PROGRESSION OF FOODS

Keep in mind that all babies grow and develop at different rates. Never accept textbook-style advice about when to begin what food. There have been numerous theories about infant feeding over the past few decades including the trend of bottle feeding rather than breast-feeding, which was still prevalent until the late sixties. The baby's parents should be the informed decision makers and the Nanny's role is to provide information about how the baby responds to feedings and also to provide information gained from personal experience and education.

Some pediatricians have recommended that infants be given only breast milk or formula for the first year of life to prevent obesity or for other reasons. However good this advice may be for some babies who are completely satisfied with this diet, it may not be best for all babies. Many infants have done well and have been satisfied taking cereal during the first months of life, especially large birth-weight babies.

There is a misconception that offering food each time the baby fusses will result in the baby becoming obese. This could occur if the only comfort the infant knows is food. However, if the baby is rocked, talked to, snuggled and generally well cared for emotionally and other methods of comforting the baby are used consistently, obesity should not be a concern. Healthy babies who are well cared for both emotionally and physically will not overeat.

The next type of food could be strained applesauce. Always give new foods (or juices) one at a time. Never introduce more than one new food or juice at the same time since it could be difficult for the baby's digestive system. Also, the possibility of allergies should be taken into consideration, and introducing more than one food at a time reduces your ability to determine which food may be the culprit if a food reaction presents itself.

The baby's parents and pediatrician will decide when to switch from formula to cow's milk, and how to do so slowly and gradually. NEVER switch abruptly from formula to all cow's milk. First, we have to find out whether the baby can tolerate cow's milk at all, even in diluted form. Then we can gradually give it in a more concentrated form.

Spoon Feeding Guidelines

Use a long-handled baby spoon. Fill it 1/2 with the mixture and gently put it into the baby's mouth. Let the baby suck the spoon. You cannot use the same feeding technique as with older children because sucking is the only type of feeding of which the baby is capable. The first solid feeding may be quite messy. But after the second or third feeding the baby will learn, and solid food will really be satisfying. The first solid food should be given at night because it is very filling for the baby and eating is hard work. The chances are that the baby will sleep longer than usual afterwards. Since we are trying to get the infant on a regular sleep schedule, we'll want the baby to sleep the longest during the nighttime hours rather than during the day.

Establishing The Child's Food Likes And Dislikes As A Guide

In planning the menu, it is essential to first establish what the child likes and does not like. We all have heard of the well-meaning parent, aunt or grandmother insisting that we "clean our plate" regardless of whether or not we liked what was on it! We must ALWAYS determine what the child enjoys and try to incorporate that into a balanced diet. It is our job to see that the children in our care are well nourished with the foods they like to eat. There may be times when we will need to actively encourage children to eat a proper diet. This will take a little creativity. Make a list of what children like and do not like. From this list, prepare a proper menu utilizing the correct number of servings from the Food Pyramid. Pay attention to any dietary restrictions or family restrictions, e.g., health foods. It is also essential that the plate be attractive. Do not mix foods together that are on the same plate. When preparing meals for children with poor appetites, never pile food on the plate, as this will diminish the appetite even further.

Ask a family member how they like food prepared. Acknowledge any cultural differences or customs the family may have. Kosher households may use certain bowls or dishes for meats and others for breads and cereals. Respect and follow the preferences of the individual or family you are helping. Proper nourishment is the goal in meal planning and the best way to accomplish this is by following the methods of eating your family prefers.

Reminder: people have their own tastes. Prepare meals the way the child or child's family enjoys them. Don't impose your own tastes on the family or child.

Eating Habits And How To Establish Them

Eating should be an enjoyable experience. Don't nag. Don't be too aggressive. Food should not be a main topic of conversation. It should not be used as a reward or as a punishment. The child should be HUNGRY and the food good tasting. Don't push milk. Too much milk takes away the appetite. After 1 year of age, milk consumption should be 20 ounces or less a day. Other fluids such as water and juices are fine. Starting at about 10 months of age let the child feed himself or herself. Of course, you should help the child finish. At first it will be kind of messy, but practice is necessary. There could be several foods that the child really hates—don't push those.

Appetite

Toddlers and older children may demonstrate erratic changes in appetite. This is normal. Again, never force children to eat something they do not like or to eat when they are not hungry. Some children may go an entire day or longer without eating and still be perfectly healthy. Continue to observe the child and if the loss of appetite is accompanied by fever or other symptoms or if it continues beyond a day or two, call the pediatrician. Be certain that the child is not filling up on "junk" foods. This may be the reason behind the loss of appetite. Junk foods should be avoided completely and should not be used as a reward.

Any concerns regarding the child's nutritional intake should be discussed with the pediatrician. The doctor will compare the child's growth and development with both the child's individual history and the "norms" for the child's age and sex. Keep careful notes on nutritional intake in your daily log, so that you can assess the child's overall nutritional status regularly. Look for eating patterns that may omit certain food groups or patterns that include too much of one and not enough of another. Adjust the menu as needed. It is not unusual, at times, for a child to favor one particular food at the exclusion of almost anything else. Enthusiastically encourage variety but never force the child to eat.

Food Attitudes

Children will mimic attitudes toward certain foods. Example: A twelve-year-old is feeding an eight-month-old sibling an assorted dish of baby food consisting of strained peas, strained beef and strained prunes. Throughout the meal, the twelve-year-old comments on how "yucky" the food is, how "awful" it smells and proceeds to attempt to feed the infant while making no attempt to disguise the look of disgust.

Although this is an exaggerated example, don't believe for a second that even an infant is unaware of your attitude toward the food you have on the plate. Infants understand a lot more than most people give them credit for. Just because their verbal skills are not well developed does not mean they don't understand much or all of what is said.

The Nannies who understand the impact they may have in the development of good nutritional habits will talk enthusiastically about the good food they are offering. The knowledgeable Nannies will also talk about how delicious fruit is, what pretty colors the apples, oranges and plums are, and will refrain from snacking on junk foods anytime a child is present. Fruit should always be available for snacking and it is a good idea to have it where it can be seen, e.g., on the counter or table.

This is how good habits begin. Don't be concerned about the child "missing out" on candy or other kinds of treats. All children will have plenty of opportunities to get well acquainted with junk foods at birthday parties and other social gatherings. However, children in the infancy and/or toddler-hood age levels with a conscientious Nanny to care for them may be at the stage when they will have the only opportunity to get the right start when it comes to developing good nutritional habits.

STOCKING THE LUNCH BOX

There is a great temptation to gravitate toward fast, processed foods for the child's lunch box, especially when your child tells you that lunch box contents are a commodity in the cafeteria and are regularly traded with classmates. One way to reduce the amount of "cafeteria trading" is to stock your child's lunch box with anything but packaged fast foods. Chances are that few of your child's classmates will trade a twinkie for baby carrots with dip, an apple, or cheese & crackers!

BREADS AND GRAINS—This category can be rounded out with things other than sandwiches. Rolls with portion-sized jelly packs are a good choice. The more nutritious crackers are a good idea. Some children like bagels, pita bread or muffins. All of these are good choices when it comes to being sure your child is getting what they need in this food category. Some children will enjoy bread sticks or rice cakes and the variety makes them more appealing. This food group is the best source of time-released energy and will keep blood-sugar levels more consistent than most other food choices. This means they will feel more awake and alert at school. Plus the complex carbohydrates and fiber helps control weight because this group tends to be more filling than others.

FRUITS AND VEGETABLES—Raisins, dried fruits, melon slices, apples, oranges and any other fresh fruit your child enjoys is a good choice. Bananas are not always a great idea because they tend to turn brown in the lunch-box and don't look appealing. Also easy and convenient are carrot sticks, celery sticks, and, for the vegetable lover, cut up fresh broccoli and cauliflower with a yogurt dip. Unsweetened fruit juices can also be substituted. These groups are interchangeable to a certain extent provided there is variety. Each provides low-fat, high-fiber nutrition rich in a variety of vitamins, potassium and iron.

MILK AND MILK PRODUCTS—These foods are rich in calcium as well as other vitamins and minerals needed for the development of strong bones and teeth. Good lunchbox choices include cheese slices, cheese sticks, yogurt, puddings and milk drinks. Add some money to your child's lunch-box if the school sells ice milk or frozen yogurt for dessert.

PROTEIN—Hard-boiled eggs, peanut-butter sandwiches, peanut-butter crackers, a few ounces of seeds or nuts are the healthiest choices. Tuna fish or very low-fat deli meat may be good choices for children who enjoy these foods. Choose a whole-wheat roll or high-fiber bread if you are making sandwiches. If you use condiments, use them sparingly. Children who have grown accustomed to only small amounts of additives are very satisfied and will most likely maintain a low consumption of empty calories throughout their lives.

CHAPTER THIRTEEN

Hygiene

BATHING

As soon as the baby arrives home for the hospital, he/she can be sponge-bathed daily. You will not immerse the baby in water in a tub bath until the umbilicus is completely healed, and the "stump" has fallen off (approximately 2 weeks). Also, baby boys who have been circumcised must not be immersed in water until the penis has completely healed (2-3 weeks).

Equipment

Sponge "tub pad"—to place inside sink or inside infant size tub. Tub pads, approximately two feet in length and five inches in depth, and were originally designed to be used in conjunction with plastic infant tubs. However, many people buy only the tub pad and place it in the sink.

Two (2) infant wash cloths, or preferably better quality paper towels (i.e., Bounty) which are not as bulky as standard washcloths, and made of softer material.

Baby shampoo—non-stinging baby shampoo should always be used rather than any other kind to prevent stinging should soap get into baby's eyes. Note: no other additional "baby soap" is needed as most are very similar to shampoo.

Large terry towel—baby size towels or towels with hoods are not as practical as an adult size terry towel when it comes to drying the baby off, especially in cold weather. They are also more absorbent.

Procedure

1. Room temperature should be at least 70 ° degrees Fahrenheit.
2. Put all of the above within easy reach of the sink.
3. Never leave the baby unattended on changing table, in tub, or on counter.

After thoroughly cleaning the sink, place the "tub pad" inside with the more heavily padded end on the side where baby's head will be placed or the pad can be placed inside an infant tub. (Note: the tub pad is longer than most sinks. This is fine as it will provide more of a cushion for baby's head.)

Turn water on, adjust to get the proper temperature (should be tepid). Leave water running with faucet adjusted to the far side of the sink away from baby.

Reminder: *Bath water should be tepid—neither hot nor cold to the touch. Baby's delicate skin can easily be burned in water temperatures that are tolerated easily by adults.*

Place bath towel on changing table or counter.

- Undress baby (baby boys have a tendency to urinate when their diaper is removed! Keep a cloth diaper or small towel over penis). Clean diaper area as you would when changing diapers.
- Keep up a soothing dialogue with baby at bath time. This will relax her and is important in establishing bath time as a pleasant experience.

- Feel water for proper temperature (tepid). Water should not be running near baby but on far side of sink.
- Place baby on tub pad.
- Use the wet paper towel or cloth without soap to gently wipe off eye lids from the inner corner close to the nose to the out corner.
- Check water temperature frequently while it is running.
- Wipe off head with wet cloth, intermittently squeezing water onto the head. Use the scalp brush gently if skin on head is dry and flaky.
- Place a dime size amount of baby shampoo on baby's head and lather, rinse.
- Wash face with cloth. Do not use soap.
- Squeeze excess water from cloth and wash in and around ears into ear canal only as far as your index finger can reach. **DO NOT put Q-tips or anything else inside baby's ear canal.**
- Wash neck and shoulders and armpits and under skin folds.
- Wash arms, hands, and in between fingers.
- Wash back and chest, keeping water away from unhealed umbilicus.
- Wash legs, feet, and in between toes. Be certain to get cloth or paper towel in between all skin folds.
- Place a drop of soap (baby shampoo is fine) on cloth and wash diaper area: Always wash front first. Avoid getting circumcised penis wet—do not wash. Wash buttocks and anal area last.
- Now use the second washcloth or paper towel to rinse diaper area thoroughly.
- Remove baby from tub. HOLD FIRMLY—wet babies are slippery. Place on bath towel. Dry baby thoroughly in the same order he/she was washed (head to toe, diaper area last).
- After umbilicus falls off and circumcision heals, you can fill the tub 1/4 full with tepid water when bathing.
- Umbilicus care—(see Common Concerns) for equipment and procedure.

Reminder: *Never leave baby unattended when on changing table, on counter, or in bath.*

SKIN CARE

Unless baby has dry flaky skin, baby lotions, powder and/or oils are unnecessary. If baby's skin is dry, do the following:

- Use a drop or two of baby oil.
- Rub into your hands.
- Massage into baby's skin.

DIAPERING

- Wipe off any excess with dry towel.
- If scalp is dry or flaky do allow a small amount of excess oil to remain on scalp if scales or crusted areas are present.
- Repeat procedure four times a day.
- In very warm weather use corn starch instead of powder in all skin folds and diaper area.
- Change baby's position frequently while he/she is unable to turn over himself approximately every hour or more often if he/she indicates, i.e., if baby looks uncomfortable.
- Place all necessary items within reach:

  1) Clean diaper.
  2) 2 or 3 warm paper towels (the commercial baby "wipes" are usually cold on baby's delicate skin). The better quality paper towels will not fall apart when wet. They are soft, and ideal for baby care.
  3) Small hand towel for under baby's bottom.
  4) Desitin lotion if rash present.

5) Wash baby with wet paper towels "front to back." [Note: genitals always washed first, anal area last. This prevents the "E Coli" bacteria present in feces from entering the urethra which could result in a urinary tract infection.]
6) Dry diaper area thoroughly.
7) Open clean diaper and place taped end under buttocks.
8) Bring other end between legs.
9) Fold top edge of diaper inside, below umbilicus area.

Note: With premature or very tiny babies you may want to make the diaper smaller by cutting several inches off this edge before you start to diaper baby to prevent friction of diaper against umbilicus.

There is no need to use baby powder except in warm weather. Then cornstarch should be used, which is natural and does not contain the perfumes, etc. found in commercial powders.

Lotions need not be used routinely unless skin is dry or a rash is present. Desitin is a good choice for mild diaper rash, however, it is always a good idea to check with your pediatrician regarding a rash.

Change diaper approximately every two hours.

Be certain diaper is not too tight. You should be able to fit your fingers comfortably inside to—otherwise it's too tight.

Diapering baby boys: Even after umbilicus falls off continue to fold top end of diaper under before taping in pace—(not necessary with baby girls). This is to prevent urine from shooting out the top of the diaper which can only occur with male children because of their anatomical structure.

Note: *When removing soiled diaper, place a small hand towel over penis, should baby urinate before new diaper is in place. This often does occur*

NAIL CARE

While some babies need their finger nails trimmed as soon as they're born, with others it may be several weeks before nails need to be cut. It's important to check nails daily since baby may scratch herself. Toe nails are usually not long enough to be cut for several months, however, they too should be checked routinely. The best time to cut nails is while baby is sleeping.

Equipment

Child size nail clipper (scissors have pointed tips which could injure a squirming baby).

Procedure

Cut straight across—do not cut sides near cuticle. Be certain not to leave ragged edges.

DRESSING

Part of the daily dressing routine should include applying sunscreen, regardless of the season.

When buying clothing, always buy sizes 2-3 months "older" than the age of your child, i.e., buy 3 month sizes for newborns, otherwise baby may only wear them once.

Infants grow at a very fast rate and many times do not even have the opportunity to wear all the clothing bestowed on them by fiends, relatives, and parents before they grow out of them.

Therefore, it is wise to be practical especially since most infants are sleeping and eating most of the time anyway. An infant's wardrobe should include:

- Disposable diapers (buy in quantity), or cloth
- Tee shirts that snap in crotch—10

- Sleepers—10
- Socks—5 (avoid booties that tie at ankle, choose a thick, longer baby sock instead. It will keep baby's feet warmer and will not fall off, or cut off circulation)
- Sweaters—2
- Outdoor wear appropriate to the season
- Bibs—10

Guidelines

- Dress the baby according to how you would dress yourself in terms of warmth.
- In cold weather babies lose body heat more quickly than adults. Both socks and a hat (a lot of body heat is lost through the head) are helpful and will keep baby comfortable).
- Dress baby in layers of clothing in cold weather, rather than just a heavy sweater.
- Keep baby out of direct sun during mid-day, especially in hot weather.
- Feel baby's skin under clothing to determine if baby is warm enough, too warm, etc.
- Infants and especially newborns will have cold hands and feet which is no necessarily an indication of being cold in general. It is just that the infant's circulation is not as efficient as an adult's.
- Clothes should be loose fitting, not snug. You should not have to struggle to get clothing on or off.
- Most babies will not lie still and cooperate when being dressed. This is not a reflection on you or your ability. It helps a lot to keep up a soothing dialogue with baby while you are dressing him.
- Get into the habit of always dressing baby in clothes that are color coordinated and that match. Although baby won't notice, others (parents) will take note of how well dressed baby is.

Parents have found it disconcerting to have the color coordinated outfits they have purchased ignored while baby is outfitted in mismatched clothing. The way their child is dressed may be as important to them as how they, themselves are dressed—be sensitive to this.

- Stained clothing should not be worn unless necessary.
- Always remove expensive clothing before feeding baby or use a large bib.
- Avoid (whenever possible) clothing that is lacy, or ornamental. It is usually not as comfortable.
- All clothing should be "flame resistant." Check the label to be sure since clothing bought in foreign countries or some designer clothes may not be. **These should not be worn.**

Other Grooming Considerations

Hair care—if baby's hair is long as is the case with some babies, it should be neat and may even require a trim. (Never cut hair on any child without checking with parents first!) Style the hair.

General cleanliness—always keep baby's face clean. Change baby anytime he/she spits up on clothing.

Hygiene Considerations As Baby Grows

A plastic ring with suction cups on bottom, which attaches to sink or tub, sometimes called a "babysitter" can be used with babies 5 months and older once they are able to sit up pretty well. These allow baby to splash and play while your hands are free to wash baby. It may be helpful to place a washcloth under baby's bottom to prevent baby from sliding and also for comfort.

Older children can use the tub for their daily bath. Always take child out of tub or off of counter/changing table to answer door, telephone, or to check on another child.

DENTAL HYGIENE

By the time your child has reached his 2'nd birthday he/she is ready for his first visit to the dentist. Assist parents in choosing a dentist who has a pediatric dental practice and who comes well recommended. It is important that a child's first dental visit be relaxed and uneventful. Be very certain not to relay any negative feelings you may have about seeing the dentist. This can cause a child to fear going, not to mention the unnecessary anxiety that your child could needlessly experience, this could effect his dental health for years to come since people who fear dental visits avoid going.

Prior to the teeth erupting wipe the infant's gums with a soft wash cloth or a piece of gauze (baby won't enjoy this!) every day. The reason behind this is that even though the teeth haven't erupted, bacteria is present in the mouth. Formula residue, pacifier residue, whatever baby may have put in his mouth etc., all add bacteria to the mouth. The American Dental Association did a study several years ago in which they routinely cleaned the gums of infants before their teeth erupted. What they found is that babies whose gums were clean had little to no teething pain as their first teeth erupted. The theory is that bacteria on the splitting gums cause inflammation & teething pain.

How To Clean Baby's Teeth

Use a piece of gauze or damp wash cloth to help remove plaque at bath time, from birth until teeth have erupted, at which time you may introduce a soft bristle toothbrush.

Preventing Dental Disease

Never put baby to bed with a bottle. Not only is it dangerous, i.e., choking, but liquids like milk, formula and apple/orange/grape juices can cause "nursing bottle syndrome" which is a dental disease that rots the baby's teeth, causing them to crumble. This may first appear as white spots on the teeth which may later turn them yellow or brown. Early detection can prevent further decay, not to mention a lot of discomfort on baby's part.

It is the Nanny's responsibility to care for her child's teeth until about the age of 7. Preschoolers and young school age children are not yet ready to care for their teeth properly.

The Proper Toothbrush

Buy a child size brush with soft bristles that don't scratch gums. Never use a brush with hard bristles.

The Proper Way To Brush

The proper way to brush is to hold the toothbrush at a 45 ° angle facing bristles where the gum line ends and tooth begins. This will help loosen and remove harmful bacteria before it is lodged under the gums. Brush all teeth surfaces thoroughly and both sides and top.

Set A Good Example

Children will learn better if you illustrate the procedure for them. You can brush your teeth at the same time while the child watches you. Children love to imitate grown-ups and you can get them to help with this important hygiene task at the same time.

Before Visiting The Dentist

- Prepare the child by explaining the visit in a very simple conversation, as in "Oh by the way…"
- "The dentist is the tooth doctor and we have to go for a checkup."
- "You'll sit in a Mommy (Daddy) size chair that can move up and down so the dentist can look in your mouth."

Prevention Is Half The Battle

Do not give the child soft drinks, candy (especially sticky candy like licorice, taffy, etc.) Get in the habit of providing snacks like fresh fruit and vegetables early in life. Check teeth and clean at least daily as soon as the first tooth appears. Ask the doctor about fluoride drops if your own town water does not contain it.

Checklist And Points Of Emphasis for Older Children Bathing

- Toddlers and children up to the age of seven or so should have a routine bath time. Before bed is a good time since bath time can be relaxing.
- Check water temperature before placing child in tub. It should be tepid (neither hot nor cold to the touch.)
- Do not leave any child alone when bathing.
- When older children start to bath independently, keep up a dialogue with them if you are not in the bathroom. You can be available to assist them, give them some privacy and be certain they are all right all at the same time.
- Never allow children to roughhouse in the tub, shower, or bathroom.
- It is not necessary to wash a child's hair every day unless it's obvious that it needs it. Three times a week is fine.
- Observe the same general equipment and procedural guidelines for older children as your would with infants, omitting the obvious.

SKIN CARE

When teaching proper hygiene habits, emphasize cleaning (and wiping) perineal area ("bottom") from front to back, so that feces does not enter the urethra which could cause a urinary tract infection.

Skin care is not usually a great concern with older children unless they have been in the sun, have insect bites or poison ivy, oak, etc.

Sun Exposure: A tepid bath with a tablespoon of baking soda added is soothing to sunburned skin. Don't allow the child to remain in tub too long since it can be drying (natural oils removed). Lotion is also soothing—never use lotion and oil together. It can clog pores. Protect child from over-exposure to sun by using unblock lotion 15.

Insect Bites: Tepid bath with baking soda can also sooth irritated skin and decrease itching. Calamine lotion can be used after bath.

Poison Ivy/Oak: Depending on severity, a sponge bath may be more appropriate to prevent spreading. Apply calamine lotion to reduce itch. Ask pediatrician for antipyretic (anti-itch) medication to take especially before bedtime to reduce itching and spread, if severe.

NAIL CARE

Nails should be cut after bathing since they will be softer, thus easier to trim.

Ask child to "scratch" the soap by dragging fingernails across the soap bar. This will get the soap under the nails and make them easier to clean.

Always check nails for cleanliness before each meal and before leaving the house to go anywhere.

DRESSING

As with infants, applying sunscreen should be part of the daily routine, regardless of the season.

Clothes are the Nanny's responsibility in terms of laundering and ironing unless a housekeeper or maid is employed.

Clothes should always match, fit well, and be in good condition (not torn or stained).

Let parents know when child needs his wardrobe replenished.

Check shoe fit by asking child to push his toe against your finger while he/she has shoe on and you are feeling the edge of the shoe. Be certain to have shoe size checked every 3 to 6 months by a qualified children's shoe sales person.

HAIR CARE

Hair should always be clean and neat. Long hair should be styled.

DENTAL CARE

Brush before bath since saliva, toothpaste, etc. can end up on child's face and chest.

BOOKS FOR CHILDREN ABOUT HYGIENE;

Clean Enough by K. Henkes

Germs Make Me Sick" by P. Donahue

Morris Has A Cold by B. Wiseman

CHAPTER FOURTEEN

Common Pediatric Illnesses

CARING FOR CHILDREN WHO ARE ILL

Anytime you have a question or concern about the health of any child left in your care, you should discuss it at once with either another knowledgeable adult, or with the pediatrician.

If your concerns are related to problems at the level of teething pain or a minor rash, the child's parents or a relative may be able to evaluate the situation along with you. You could also discuss minor concerns the nurse in the Pediatrician's office. Other concerns such as difficulty breathing or an elevated temperature require the input of the Pediatrician immediately. In the sure whether or not the child is seriously hurt, always have the child seen by a physician or at least call the pediatrician to discuss the situation.

In any case, it is always best to follow up on any concerns or questions you have with the appropriate person. Never attempt to diagnose or treat an illness or injury on your own.

The following information is intended for the purpose of increasing your level of knowledge. It should never be used instead of seeking the advice of the child's pediatrician. Under the following headings you may see the terminology, incubation, and range and/or isolation.

Incubation Period—refers to the time when the illness is contagious. Unfortunately symptoms usually don't present themselves until after the incubation period. However, it makes sense to be cautious exposing siblings of the ill child if one of the children in your family has a contagious illness, since the siblings may be in the incubation period of the same illness.

Range—length of illness (average).

Isolation—means that the illness is contagious while symptoms are present. Isolate from other children.

General guideline for sick children;—never give aspirin to anyone less than 20 years old (Reyes Syndrome)

THRUSH

A form of fungi that looks like dried on milk on lips and inside of mouth, especially inside cheeks and roof of mouth. Call pediatrician for medication. Do not attempt to rub it off.

ROSEOLA

(Incubation period average—4 days—Isolation: when fever is present.). Roseola rash follows approximately four days of high fever (103-105 °F). It is difficult to diagnose, however, until the rash appears—flat red spots. Infant Tylenol drops are usually ordered to comfort the elevated temperature. The infant should be observed for other symptoms. Activity as tolerated.

EAR INFECTION

Ear infections are common in young children and are characterized by the infant "tugging" or "pulling" on their ear. Symptoms can include fever, chills, runny nose, fussiness, insomnia, hearing loss. Call physician for advice. Most likely the child will need to see the Pediatrician.

EPIDEMIC DIARHHEA OF NEWBORN
(Incubation period—6-7 days—Range 2-21 days—Isolation: Yes!)

Hydration is most important! If intravenous fluids are not ordered and the child is at home, give fluids by mouth at least every 3 hours or more often if infant shows signs of thirst. Don't force bottle if baby signals he has had enough for the time being. Good care of diaper area essential!!! Record number and appearance of stools and whether baby vomited. Check temp 2 times a day if a febrile (without fever). Take temperature under arm (Auxiliary temperature.)

HEAT STROKE

Child's skin will be hot, dry and flushed. Fever, increased pulse and possible loss of consciousness can occur. Remove excess clothing. Apply tepid clothes and *gradually* make the clothes colder. Never immerse in a cold tub or apply ice. Can be prevented by limiting activity in hot weather and encouraging fluids.

On hot days, ice cream; Popsicles and Jell-O can be used to get fluids into child (if uncooperative with large amounts of water or juices). Freeze fresh orange juice in ice trays. Lollipop sticks can be purchased in craft stores.

IMPETIGO CONTAGIOSA
(Incubation period—average less than 5 days—Isolation:
from child contact.)

Impetigo is a highly contagious, bacterial skin condition, which resembles acne and is usually found around the mouth. Impetigo is caused by exposure to staph and occurs primarily in unclean environments. A child could get impetigo if they for instance, had a fresh cut or scratch and then bathed in a bathtub that was not clean.

Maximum cleanliness. Phisohex wash for the whole family. Apply topical treatment (saline soaks, antibiotic ointment) as prescribed. If lesion larger than 1.5 inch square, systemic antibiotics are necessary. Watch family members and classmates for spreading of illness.

INFECTIOUS KERATOCONJUNCTIVITIS (pink eye)

(Incubation period average—5-7 days.) Hygiene—hand washing each time after touching the eye. Watch that child does not touch or rub eyes. Also watch child carefully AFTER application of antibiotic ointment, for vision is blurred for about 5 minutes after application. Keep child off her feet and under supervision to prevent falls.

DIABETES

Diabetes is the result of an imbalance between systemic insulin and sugar. The child will have medication, which will most likely need to be injected. The important thing to know about diabetes is that the amount of food that the child eats is converted to sugar and can create an imbalance if prescribed portions are not followed carefully. The other thing to know is that exercise burns sugar, thus creating an excess of insulin in the body. Therefore it is also important to adhere to the prescribed level of activity. Just keep in mind that to avoid diabetic shock or coma, you must be aware of the balance between insulin and sugar. Be knowledgeable about limits on diet, exercise. Be aware that exercise will burn up more calories (sugar) than usual and may result in what appears to be an insulin reaction; i.e. unusual behavior, hunger, weakness, perspiration. Insulin shock (reaction) and diabetic coma are the result of too much insulin in body or not enough. The symptoms for both are similar. Always carry hard candy, sugar cubes, etc. Make sure the child always carries an ID tag stating that he is diabetic. Anytime a child becomes unconscious, or appears to be losing consciousness, call an ambulance. Discuss with parents what protocol should be followed.

SCABIES
(Incubation period average—4-6 weeks—Isolation: from school).

A mite that burrows under the skin causes scabies. Scabies usually is spread by close contact. These mites are highly contagious and can live for up to four days without a human host, therefore, bed linens, furniture, towels and blankets can provide good hiding places for the scabies mite. Scabies cannot fly or jump, and it moves very slowly. Previously it was thought that the Scabies mite that thrives on humans was caused by contact with a pet. We know now that this is not the case. Scabies is not nearly as prevalent today, except where people live in crowded conditions. Most susceptible are children cared for in group settings, as well as those in hospitals or nursing homes. Watch for infection! Scabies can only be cured by using prescription creams. Over the counter medicines are not strong enough to kill them. Infants develop small blister-like sores on their hands and feet

Enforce meticulous cleanliness of child, his immediate environment, house & furniture Change bed linen and clothing. Apply medicine as prescribed.

COLD, SORE THROAT

Congestion, fatigue, fever, pain when swallowing are common. Runny nose and eyes. Call pediatrician for advice. Encourage fluids and rest periods. Quiet play. Use paper tissues to reduce spread. Do not allow children to drink out of same glass, etc. Wash hands frequently. Report back to doctor if not better in 2-3 days or if symptoms (i.e. difficulty breathing) become worse

INFLUENZA (Flu)
(Incubation period average—1-3 days—Isolation: in acute stage)

Immunization: Because new strains of the flu present themselves regularly, they are not routinely given unless the child has a chronic illness

Take the child's temperature 4 times a day. Give Tylenol if temperature is over 102 after consulting a physician. Record fluid intake and output. Give fluids generously. Watch for cough. Child should be kept quiet and comfortable
- Influenza may lead to pneumonia

SCARLET FEVER
(Incubation period average—2-5 days—Isolation: respiratory precautions.)

Isolation precautions for about 2 days after treatment started. For the same length of time change and wash linen. Give medicine prescribed. Control fever. Watch for peeling about 5 days after onset. Scarlet fever was very common prior to the development of antibiotics. Symptoms, course and treatment are nearly identical to that of Strep throat.

INFECTIOUS MONONUCLEOSIS
(Incubation period average 7-21 days—Range 7-15 days—Isolation: respiratory precautions.)

This disease is caused by the Epstein-Barr virus and has been called the "Kissing disease" because it is spread by direct oral contact. Fatigue, headache, sore throat and other flu-like symptoms are seen. Mental fatigue is more common in younger children and can initiate depression. Treatment involves comfort measures, as there is no cure, or specific treatment for mononucleosis. Children and adolescents are more prone to this disease than adults. Enlargement of the lymph nodes and spleen is common.

NO running around or roughhousing due to risk of rupture of the spleen. The throat is highly inflamed and raw; therefore don't give patient spicy foods, or acid foods (i.e. Italian or Mexican foods, ketchup, lemon, orange or citric juices).

MEASLES

(Incubation period average 5-9 days—Isolation: until 5 days after rash—Immunization: vaccine.)

Once responsible for as many as 450 deaths per year measles is relatively rare due to the widespread immunization program. (Two shots are necessary for a lifetime immunization). Control of fever very important!! Child will demonstrate severe cold symptoms. Once a person has had the measles they will never have them again. Seen mostly in children from under developed countries and those who have not been immunized. Watch for pneumonia which can follow measles.

EPILEPSY

Epilepsy is one of the most common Nervous System diseases caused by abnormal electrical activity in the brain, the cause of which can be different for different people. Head injury & medications are two some causes although it is not known specifically. Seizures are the most common symptom of epilepsy and are characterized by involuntary spasms of the muscles, resulting in loss of all muscle control & many times unconsciousness. High fever may also cause a person to seize, and is not the same as epilepsy, unless there has been brain damage as a result of the fever causing the seizure activity to continue.

There is no known cure for epilepsy and medication is the treatment of choice.

Supervise medication intake. If the child seizes, don't restrain, move any hard objects away from child's thrashing body movements. Call 911 if the seizure lasts more than three minutes. Do not force anything into the child's mouth. Try to protect her from falling Place a blanket or coat over child. Always get exact protocol from parents so that you will be prepared in the event of a seizure.

CHICKENPOX
Incubation period 14 to 20 days, Range 12 to 21 days, isolation until skin is clear

Cough, headache, chills are common symptoms which present themselves approximately 14 to 18 days after exposure to chickenpox. Chickenpox rash usually develops from 1 to 2 days after other symptoms have started. One of the most common complications of chickenpox is skin infection because the rash is itchy. Babies typically have an easier time most likely because they still have some immunity from their mother. Adults can have a very difficult time to chickenpox in many times require hospitalization. The child is contagious with chickenpox even before the rash presents itself. It's very difficult to stop the spread of chickenpox once it's gotten started. Day-care centers, schools and other highly populated areas are most prone to the spread of chickenpox. A vaccine is available. As with measles, once a person has had chickenpox they will not get them again.

As the child recovers, watch for lethargy which may be the first sign of Reyes syndrome.

GERMAN MEASLES
Incubation period average 16-18 days—Range 10-21 days—Isolation: for first week.

German measles is a mild illness that causes skin rash, fever and swollen glands. Extremely rare since national MMR immunization program. Disease is very mild, no specific care necessary. Patient should stay away from pregnant women as if a woman contracts German measles during the first trimester she can pass the disease on to her infant causing birth defects.

APPENDICITIS

Is caused by an inflammation of the appendix, a small section of bowel that has no known function. Appendicitis is characterized by lower right sided abdominal pain starting around the naval, elevated temperature and nausea and vomiting in some cases. Don't give anything to eat or drink. Call pediatrician for instructions immediately or go to the nearest emergency room. Appendicitis is most common in people ten to 30 years old. It is unusual for an infant or small child have appendicitis. The only cure is surgery to remove the ruptured appendix. If left untreated, the ruptured appendix can cause peritonitis, a life-threatening condition

CROUP
Range 2-5 days

Croup is most common in children six months to four years old. It is a virus that affects the throat and airway, causing a cough that sounds like a bark, & difficult, noisy breathing. Use a humidifier to keep the air moist. Call the pediatrician immediately for advice. Croup usually develops after the child has had a cold. The cough is worse at night, and generally improves every night thereafter. The If child's room is adjoined by a bathroom, open doors and turn on hot water in show to generate steam if humidifier is not available.

REYES SYNDROME

Much has been discussed about Reyes syndrome which affects primarily six to 12-year-old children. It is rare to see Reyes syndrome in anyone older than 18 years old. In fact, this illness has become quite rare in United States. It affects the brain and the liver. It is most often seen after the child has recovered from a recent viral infection. They have been numerous instances where aspirin was given to children during an illness and subsequently the child developed Reyes syndrome. That is why it is recommended that children under the age of 20 not receive aspirin. Reyes syndrome is not contagious, its cause is unknown & if caught early enough the child can make a complete recovery.

REGULAR HEARING TESTS—ALL AGES

Few activities are more important in caring for a child than regular testing for hearing losses. For example, the six month old is about to enter a crucial learning period, and should he fail to hear well for long periods of time, he will fail to learn language as well as he might otherwise. To the extent that language learning is negatively affected during the first years, so too is the development of higher mental abilities. To the extent that both processes suffer, the child also will be hindered with respect to social development.

While babies with profound hearing loss usually are identified very early in life, those with mild to moderate losses often are not identified until they enter school. Child Care Professionals should be on guard for warning signs throughout the child's early years. The following chart will aid you in monitoring the child's progress.

MONITORING A CHILD'S HEARING

AGE	DANGER SIGNALS
Birth to 3 months	Baby is not startled by sharp clap within three to six feet; he is not soothed by mother's or Child Care Professional's voice
3 to 6 months	Doesn't search for source of sound by turning his eyes and head; doesn't respond to mother's or Child Care Professional's voice; doesn't initiate own noises; doesn't enjoy sound-making toys
6 to 10 months	Doesn't respond to own name or to telephone ringing or to someone's voice when it is not loud; unable to understand words such as "no" and "bye-bye"
10 to 15 months	Cannot point to or look at familiar objects or people when asked to do so; cannot imitate simple words or sounds
15 to 18 months	Unable to follow simple spoken directions; does not seem to be able to expand understanding of words
Any Age	Does not awaken or is not disturbed by loud sounds; does not respond when called; pays no attention to ordinary noises; uses gestures almost exclusively to establish needs rather than verbalizing

If you suspect that the child does not hear everything he should, insist of an examination by a pediatric audiologist. Whenever a sign of hearing loss is detected, careful diagnosis and follow-up are imperative.

HOW TO READ THE THERMOMETER

It is rare these days to see a mercury thermometer used in the home. However, there are still some in use and you should be familiar with the correct procedure, ask someone to practice with you until you are comfortable. It is essential that you be completely at ease with this procedure. Your local Visiting Nurse Association can teach you and is probably your best resource if you are not enrolled in a formal training program. Many homes now have modem thermometers, which are non-evasive, or digital. The following is provided for those using a mercury thermometer and/or a simple digital.

*Be certain when disposing of a mercury thermometer, call your local board of health for instructions. Mercury is harmful to the environment.

When to Take Temperature

You should take a child's temperature anytime you suspect a fever, when he feels warm, is fussy for no apparent reason or shows other unusual symptoms. A reading of or above 101 is considered elevated. Call the physician and continue to assess the child by taking her temperature again in 2 hours, or sooner if she appears to be feeling worse. Continue to take the temperature every 2-4 hours as long as the temperature remains elevated.

Ways to Take the Temperature when only a mercury thermometer is at hand

Body temperature is measured with a thermometer. Although the majority of households with small children have a digital thermometer on hand—which is simple to use—there are nevertheless some households that still use the mercury thermometers. There are three ways to take a temperature: orally (by mouth), auxiliary (under the arm pit), and rectally (by rectum). The most accurate of these methods is rectally. You would use the rectal route for infants and children under the age of three or anytime the child is uncooperative. The oral route can be used for routine readings on children who are cooperative.

Normal Body Temperature

The normal body temperature is 98.6°, although some people may have slightly higher or lower temperatures. As you gain experience in taking temperatures you will notice that if you were to take the temperature of a child by mouth, and then by rectum, the rectal reading will be one degree higher. This is why we say that the rectal route is more accurate. Always state which route was used when reporting a child's temperature. For example, 98.6° P0 means 98.60 by mouth (P0). IF the reading is by rectum, it should be written as 99.60 R (the R indicating rectal). An auxiliary reading would be written as 98.6° AX. Never take a temperature by mouth and add on another degree, simply state, which was used.

Reporting to the Physician or Parent

If at any time, a child's temperature reaches or exceeds 101°, it should be reported immediately to the pediatrician. This reading may indicate the beginning of a serious infection requiring medical attention. Many households now have digital thermometers which came with specific instructions. If you are using a mercury thermometer, the following instructions will be helpful.

How Long to Leave Thermometer In

When taking a temperature by mouth or by rectum, leave the thermometer in place at least three (3) minutes. The auxiliary route requires from three (3) to five (5) minutes.

Procedure for Rectal Temperature—Infants and Toddlers

1. Shake the thermometer down below 96°, lubricate end with Vaseline or oil.

2. Place the child on his/her back on a safe comfortable surface.
3. Lift buttocks off surface by grasping ankles as you would if you were changing a diaper.
4. While child's buttocks are lifted, insert clean, lubricated thermometer into rectum, approximately 1/2 to 1 inch. **NOTE: Never force the thermometer!** If you meet resistance, stop and use another route to take the temp.
5. Divert the child's attention by talking to him/her during the procedure.
6. Remove, wipe off and read.
7. Write down reading, notify pediatrician if temp is 101° or above.
8. Wash the thermometer in alcohol or with soap and water, dry, put in proper place.

Never take a rectal temperature on a child with diarrhea—use the auxiliary route.

Procedure for Rectal Temperature— Children Who Can Follow Directions:

1. Shake the thermometer down below 96°, lubricate end with Vaseline or oil.
2. Turn the child on his/her side. Be certain to provide privacy!
3. Insert the thermometer into the rectum. Do not leave the child alone, continue to hold the end of the thermometer. **If you cannot easily insert the thermometer, do not force.** Report this to the pediatrician and take the reading using one of the other two routes.
4. Remove after three (3) minutes, wipe off with tissue and read. Record the reading, report any significant data.
5. Wash the thermometer in alcohol and tepid water, put in proper place.

Procedure for Oral Temperature

1. Shake the thermometer with three (3) or more brisk jerks of the hand. (Be certain never to interchange one thermometer between the mouth, and the rectum).
2. Once the mercury is below 96º, place it under the child's tongue.
3. Leave in place for at least three (3) minutes.
4. Wash the thermometer with alcohol and tepid water, dry and put in proper place.
5. Wash your hands.
6. Record the reading in the proper place.
7. If the child has a fever, make a notation that the temperature should be re-taken in three (3) hours.
8. Notify the pediatrician if the reading is 101º or greater.
9. If the child has had something hot or cold to drink, or has been running around or overly excited, wait 15 minutes before taking the temperature.

Procedure for Auxiliary Temperature

1. Shake the thermometer down below 96 ºF.
2. Place under the armpit.
3. Leave in place for three (3) to five (5) minutes. Be certain that the child is holding his arm against his body so the instrument will not fall out.
4. Remove and read.
5. Record and report significant data.

What to Do If Child Has a Temperature

Encourage fluids and give Tylenol if the physician orders it. Never give aspirin unless the doctor specifically orders aspirin. Keep the child as quiet as possible. Retake the temperature every 2-4 hours until it subsides. Convulsions can occur when a child has an elevated temperature.

MEDICATIONS

Anytime medication is prescribed for a child in your care, it is absolutely essential that you are certain of the following:

ACTION; What is the medicine's action? What is it supposed to do, help, relieve? (If it's a pain or analgesic medication, its action is to relieve pain, etc.) You need to know this so you can observe the effectiveness of the medication and inform the parents and or the pediatrician.

AMOUNT: How many pills, (capsules, teaspoons) is the child supposed to receive?

STRENGTH: What is the strength, i.e. 2 milligram pills, 4 milligrams? This is especially important if the medication is increased or decreased, or if the pediatrician orders four milligrams (4 mgs.). Every (4) four hours and the pharmacy sends 2 milligram tablets. (In this case, you would give two pills every four hours in order to comply with the doctor's request.) Most pharmacies provide the exact dosage

WHEN TO GIVE MEDICATION: Some medication such as antibiotics need to reach and maintain what's called a "blood level" meaning so much of the medication has to be circulating in the body in order for it to work. Always give according to what the doctor prescribes, exactly. Write it down each time you give it. Always use a Medication Chart like the EZ-DOSE-IT chart at the end of this chapter when giving medication to enhance communication between parent & nanny. Give it on time.

SIDE EFFECTS;

Almost every medication has one or more side effects. Feel free to call the pharmacy and ask to speak to a pharmacist and ask him what the side effects are with the particular medication. They usually are more up to date about medications than the doctor and they will be happy to help you. Observe child for any possible side effects and write any pertinent information in your daily log. It is also a good idea to write down the most common side effects directly on your Medication Chart for each medication given.

SPECIAL INSTRUCTIONS: Some medications need to be refrigerated. Others should be stored out of direct sunlight, or damp areas, like the bathroom. Some should be taken on an empty stomach. While others need to be taken with food or milk. Pay attention to medications that will make the child drowsy, as falls are a possibility & lack of coordination.

LIQUID MEDICATION: will be dispensed with either a spoon, or a dropper. Liquids droppers are often measured in cc's (cubic centimeters). Sometimes for instance, a medication will indicate that there are 5mg per cc. If the prescription says 10mg 3 times a day, you will give 2 cc's. If the order said 2.5 mg, you would give one half of a cc. Be certain you are giving the correct dosage and always ask if you have any questions whatsoever.

ACCURATE DOCUMENTATION: Maintain a medication charting system, like the "Easy Dose-it" medication sheets, anytime a child is receiving medication. Keep the chart on the fridge, or in another conspicuous place. Write down each dose and make notes about any significant observations you may have.

Anytime you are unsure about a medication order i.e. how much to give, when to give, it's action, or any special instructions, don't hesitate to call the pharmacist. Also check expiration dates, throw away any medications that no longer being used and never give medication to anyone it was not ordered for. And, of course, to begin any medicine to anyone without a prescription.

E-Z DOSE-IT®

MEDICATION CHART FOR M a r y j a n e

		Times to Be Given	Date 10/23	Date 10/24	Date 10/25	Date 10/26	Date 10/27	Date 10/28	Date 10/29	Date 10/30	Date 10/31	Date 11/01	Date
Name of Medication	**Am oxicillin**	breakfast					10A						
		lunch		2:30									
		dinner											

Special Instructions, and/or Side Effects to look for

Give 1 teaspoonful every eight hours with meals for ten days by mouth for strep throat (250 mg per teaspoon) Keep refrigerated. SIDE EFFECTS; Allergic reaction (difficulty breathing; closing of your throat; swelling of your lips, tongue, or face; or hives) headache, diarrhea or nausea, dry mouth or increased thirst, or yeast infection.

©1996 Professional Nanny

E-Z DOSE-IT®

MEDICATION CHART FOR _____

	Times to Be Given	Date	Date	Date	Date	Date	Date	Date	Date	Date	Date	Date
Name of Medication												

Special Instructions, and/or Side Effects to look for

©1996 Professional Nanny

EMERGENCY INFORMATION
911

MOTHER'S NAME_____ FATHER'S_____

FATHER'S WORK # _____ CELL # _____

MOTHER'S WORK#_____ CELL # _____

POISON CONTROL #_____

(If ever in doubt—always call & ask questions)

PEDIATRICIAN NAME_____TELEPHONE_____

ADDRESS_____

ALTERNATE'S NAME _____TELEPHONE_____

HOSPITAL_____**EMERGENCY ROOM #**_____

(if ever in doubt about the seriousness of an injury—call for advice)

AMBULANCE_____#_____

(In an emergency,call an ambulance, especially if you have more than one child to care for)

DENTIST: NAME_____#_____

ADDRESS_____

CLOSEST RELATIVE_____#_____

NEAREST NEIGHBOR_____#_____

MEDICAL INSURANCE_____#_____

SUBSCRIBER #_____GROUP #_____

DENTAL INSURANCE_____#_____

SUBSCRIBER #_____GROUP #_____

CONSENT AUTHORIZATION FORM

I, _____ the undersigned, authorize

(Parent)

_____to make decisions, in my absence,

(Nanny)

for the benefit of my child_____for whatever

(Child)

emergency medical measures are deemed necessary for the care and protection of my child.

CHILD_____DOB___/___/___SEX___HAIR___EYES___
MEDICAL CONDITIONS_____ALLERGIES_____
HEALTH INSURER_____TELEPHONE___/___/___
SUBSCRIBER_____SS#_____
PEDIATRICIAN_____TELEPHONE_____
DENTIST_____ TELEPHONE_____

CHILD_____DOB___/___/___SEX___HAIR___EYES___
MEDICAL CONDITIONS_____ALLERGIES_____
HEALTH INSURER_____TELEPHONE___/___/___
SUBSCRIBER_____SS#_____
PEDIATRICIAN_____TELEPHONE_____
DENTIST_____ TELEPHONE_____

CHILD_____DOB___/___/___SEX___HAIR___EYES___
MEDICAL CONDITIONS_____ALLERGIES_____
HEALTH INSURER_____TELEPHONE___/___/___
SUBSCRIBER_____SS#_____
PEDIATRICIAN_____TELEPHONE_____
DENTIST_____ TELEPHONE_____

Parent Signature_____Date_____

Signature witnessed by (notary)

_____Date_____

FIRST AID SUPPLY CHECKLIST

According to the American Academy of Pediatrics, parents should stock the following items in the family medicine cabinets:

- ✓ Acetaminophen for treating a child's fever
- ✓ Adhesive tape
- ✓ Antibiotic cream for use on cuts and scrapes
- ✓ Elastic bandages to support sprained ankles or other injured body parts
- ✓ Gauze bandages to cover cuts or deep wounds
- ✓ Hydrocortisone cream to soothe bug bites or poison ivy
- ✓ Cotton balls or swabs
- ✓ Plastic bandages
- ✓ Scissors—use ones with rounded ends to cut bandages
- ✓ Cold and cough medications
- ✓ Saline nose drops
- ✓ Nasal aspirator to remove mucus after administering saline nose drops
- ✓ Ipecac to induce vomiting. NOTE. Use ONLY under the advice of a physician
- ✓ Infant dosing spoon
- ✓ Rectal thermometer and Petroleum jelly to use as a lubricant
- ✓ Rubbing alcohol
- ✓ Tweezers to remove splinters

CHAPTER FIFTEEN

Managing Stress

In recent years, there has been a wealth of material written on stress. As a Nanny, it is essential that you understand and learn to cope with stressful situations. Through self-knowledge you can develop coping mechanisms and skills which will help you in dealing with stress in stressful situations whether it be the children in your care, your family or friends.

Stress is a physical, spiritual, emotional, social and intellectual response to a perceived danger or threat. Stress is not the pressure from the outside; it is the internal response to external elements. These external elements are called stressors. These stressors can be measured according to their capacity to cause stress. They often vary according to the person being affected and according to the cultural context. The "Social Readjustment" scale illustrates how different life events can impact your stress level.

THE SOCIAL READJUSTMENT RATING SCALE

1. Death of spouse   100
2. Divorce   73
3. Marital separation   65

4. Jail term   63
5. Death of close family member   63
6. Personal injury or illness   53
7. Marriage   50
8. Fired at work   47
9. Marital reconciliation   45
10. Retirement   45
11. Change in health of family member   44
12. Pregnancy   39
13. Gain of new family member   39
14. Business readjustment   39
15. Change in financial state   38
16. Death of close friend   37
17. Change to different line of work   36
18. Change in number of arguments with spouse   35
19. Mortgage over $10,000   31
20. Foreclosure of mortgage or loan   30
21. Change in responsibilities at work   29
22. Son or daughter leaving home   29
23. Trouble with in-laws   29
24. Outstanding personal achievement   28
25. Wife begins or stops work   26
26. Begin or end school   26
27. Change in living conditions   25
28. Revision of personal habits   24
29. Trouble with boss   23
30. Change in work hours or conditions   20
31. Change in residence   20
32. Change in schools   20
33. Change in recreation   19
34. Change in church activities   19
35. Change in social activities   18

36.Mortgage or loan less than $10,000	17
37.Change in sleeping habits	16
38.Change in number of family get-togethers	15
39.Change in eating habits	15
40.Vacation	13
41.Christmas	12
42.Minor violations of the law	11

POSITIVE AND NEGATIVE STRESS

Not all stress is bad. In fact, the presence of a stressor in your life may be a challenge for you to become stronger. For example, having to leave a home, friends, a situation that is known to you, for a strange place is certainly a cause of stress. When such a move occurs in order to take up a responsible job and become a responsible person, the stress involved, while still painful, can also be a cause for growth. Such a stressor can give you energy and supply new zest for living.

But stress can also become destructive. It can turn into distress when too much of it is present. It can zap your energy. It often leads to depression. Depression is often a terrifying aloneness, a psychic numbing. Life becomes quite meaningless and is robbed of its joys.

STRESS AND CHANGE

Stress is an inevitable fact of life caused by many situations and feelings, happiness, sorrow, work change, fear. One major cause of stress in one life is change. Four areas emerge as central in understanding the connection between stress and change:

1. An accumulation of change over time or a large number of changes in a brief period increases stress.
2. Both positive and negative changes are stressful.

3. Changes tend to come in clusters creating their own momen-
    tum. For example, leaving home and friends means, finding a
    new place to live, a new job and new friends.
4. Some changes consistently cause more stress than others.

Most stress occurs in what has been called "life changes," moving
from childhood, to adolescence and adulthood. Within that process we
all have fantasies of 'getting it together" in the next stage of life and we
also feel the need to hang on to "the good old days." Each life stage poses
unique development tasks. There are challenges to be met, skills to be
developed, issues to be resolved. The developmental process is often
confusing and difficult, and change often occurs before one is ready for
it. Learning to deal positively with stress and the situations which produce it can lead to improvements in one's work.

Recognizing Stress

It is important to be able to recognize harmful symptoms of stress.
Knowing what you are feeling and being able to label those feelings can
also lead to stress-reduction. The following are negative side-effects of
stress: Do any of these describe you?

✓   Irritable
✓   Unable to sleep
✓   Depressed
✓   Trembling, nervous
✓   Over-anxious
✓   Do you suffer from indigestion, headaches, fatigue, loss of
    excessive eating or increased consumption of drugs or alcohol?

These signals indicate that there is stress in your life and demand
attention.

Managing Stress

Because nothing is stressful in and of itself, the stressfulness of an event depends on how you feel about it and how you cope with it. To positively copy with the stress in your world, the following suggestions should be considered:

- ✓ Learn to tolerate what you can't change. Some problems and situations are beyond your control. Knowing what you can and cannot influence spares unnecessary anxiety.
- ✓ Exercise. Daily exercise helps you deal more effectively with stressful situations.
- ✓ Share your worries. Sometimes it helps to talk to a friend.
- ✓ Communicating your personal reaction to stress with those whom you live, work and interact will help them understand you better, thus resulting in healthier relationships.

TYPES OF STRESSORS AND THEIR EFFECTS

	SYMPTOMS	CAUSES	TREATMENT
PHYSICAL	colds, headaches, ulcers, fatigue, backaches, accidents, hypertension, sexual dysfunction	pollution, drinking, too little/much sleep, lack of exercise, bad eating habits, drinking,	posture, exercise, hypnosis, massage, relaxation, increase control of environment, slowdown, change habits; (eating, smoking, drinking, sleeping)
SPIRITUAL	grief, despair, loss of meaning,emptiness, nihilistic, hopelessness, Guilt, joylessness	doubts, bereavement, too little reflection, no commitments, Disappointment.	music, worship, learn to accept doubts, make commitment, share in grief, clarify issues, mediate.
EMOTIONAL	Depression, anxiety, Fear, happiness, loss of confidence, anger, Confusion, euphoria, Shock.	internal/external conflict, loss of esteem, failure success, lack of Stress, lack of Direction, ambiguity	accept self, sort out conflicts, assertiveness training, talk, relax, practice rational-emotive thinking, try new behavior patterns, desensitize fears, retrain reactions.
SOCIAL	Loss of friendships, Withdrawal, intimacy, loneliness, acting out, rejection, aggression, phoniness	Moving, death, vacation, change of status, change job, birth, too many people to please, marriage, pressure to conform.	find new friends, smile more, join support, group, be more honest & assertive

	Lack of creativity,	doing boring work,	find new
INTELLECTUAL	bored, loss of humor,	too little challenge,	challenges, read,
	Loss of memory, can't	materialistic values,	write, analyze,
	Concentrate, apathy,	Type A, fight to	change jobs,
	Difficulty making	succeed, too many	evaluate goals,
	Decisions	projects, lack of goals,	develop an
		Return to school	expertise

STRESS AND CHILDREN

Children have a way of letting us know when they are feeling stress by either acting out, or by withdrawing. Because children don't have the skills to deal effectively with the stress and tension in their lives—until they are taught, it is imperative that we pay attention anytime a child's behavior changes, indicating the need for caring intervention.

Environmental factors combined with a healthy imagination can create stress in children, however, this normal day-to-day kind of stress need not be enough to have a dramatic effect on a child. The determining factor has to do with how well-connected the child is to the significant adults in the child's life. An open style of communication with your child, combined with a heavy dose of authenticity, or being "real" is a potent antidote for the normal stress of daily living. By maintaining an authentic communication style, we don't mean that you give children information beyond their understanding, instead, you are honest with your child. If the Nanny is leaving and the child senses something is amiss, it makes no sense whatsoever to ignore the issue and pretend that everything is "business as usual". Likewise, if a marriage is having serious problems, it does the child no good at all to hear that everything is "fine."

It is far better for one of the parent's or another significant adult to say something like: "I bet you've noticed that Mom and Dad are not getting along very well right now." This kind of communication validates the child's feelings that something is amiss. To deny this dynamic for the sake of protecting the child is nonsense. More likely it is the adults who would rather not face the child because they either don't know how to handle it, or know that they may open a can of worms as far as how the child might react. The adult may rightly feel that they are dealing with enough already and don't want to have to bear the brunt of the child's potential reaction at the same time. Anytime a person has a feeling that something is up, yet no one will connect with them around the issue, the normal response to this is anxiety as well as a feeling of emotional alienation. This kind of denial on the part of adults teaches children NOT to trust their feelings and instincts. It cannot be stressed enough that being authentic promotes strong mental health, trust, and in the long run, helps develop coping skills, as the developing child imitates the adults style of coping and learns from it. This is the stuff that builds emotional maturity. Certainly for the adult, whether it be the Nanny, or the parent, to be able to provide this level of authenticity for a child, they must first possess it themselves.

Any behavior which deviates from your child's unusual demeanor for a day or longer should be paid attention to. Depending on the child, their response to stress may be different, however the important thing is that you stay connected, communicate authentically and provide the right example to follow by talking about how you feel on a regular basis.

ABBREVIATED LIST OF COMMON STRESSORS

Mom goes to work
New Nanny arrives
Nanny leaves
Pet ill
Pet dies
Move
New school
Start school
New teacher
Friend moves
Parents separate
Parent laid off
Parent travels
Household tension
Alcoholism
Parent/sibling illness
Family member death
Divorce
School year ends
Other life events.

Please add any items that you can think of to this list

POINTS OF EMPHASIS

During times of stress, it is especially important to communicate with the child. Otherwise, the child, whose active imagination is working overtime, will imagine the worst and become even more stressed. The following points should be kept in mind:

- Talk about what's going on (many adults try to shield children from the truth if they feel it is "inappropriate" to discuss such matters with the child. (This will only make the child feel isolated and more disconnected from the adults in her/his life.)
- Use open-ended questions as appropriate ("How do you feel about Mom being away for a week?").
- State your feelings, as appropriate ("It sure will be nice to have Mom back, the house is more organized/busy/cheerful when she's around".).
- Identify the issue innocuously, and provide opportunities for the child to express her/his feelings, or thoughts. (Remember, children will often express their feelings in one short comment and then continue with whatever activity they happen to be involved in. Don't push them for information about their feelings, just keep talking about your own.)
- Provide an environment conducive to "quiet time." "Quiet time" should be at a regularly scheduled time(s) each day, during which:

> TV should be off
> Video/radio, etc. off
> Refrain from any "busy" activities
> Turn off dishwasher, or any noisy appliance. If necessary, turn off ringer on phone.

MEDITATION AS A PREVENTATIVE MEASURE

There is a proven scientific basis for using meditation to reduce stress-related disorders. When anyone, an adult or a child, is anxious, nervous, or scared including that underlying tension we see in people who live a hectic, heavily scheduled lifestyle—that person's adrenal glands are working a lot harder than they should be. Consequently, more hormones are being pumped into the bloodstream, the heart-rate and blood pressure are higher than they would be otherwise, breathing tends to be shallow (limiting oxygen to the brain and other tissues), muscles are tense, and blood flow to vital organs decreases.

Mental relaxation via meditation stimulates the parasympatbic nervous system which counteracts these physical reactions to stress. At the Mind/Body Clinic at Deaconess Hospital, Harvard Medical School, meditation is a common and respected prescription for stress and other, more serious conditions. It is clear that meditation is utilized and widely accepted by more and more health care professionals in the medical community as the benefits of meditation become more widespread, as more people learn about it and use it.

Teach your child to meditate

Children who are familiar with meditation as a resource for coping with the everyday stress in life benefit greatly. They are calmer, and appear to be more self-assured. Probably because they are empowered with a skill which they can use independently, thus enabling them to be more self-reliant. The concept of knowing how to care for oneself competently is one of the cornerstones of high self-esteem. Children seem to benefit more when the adult uses a guided meditation tape which plays while the adult and child listen. Experienced adult mediators can lead the child via a spoken guided meditation as they meditate together. One excellent resource for introducing your child to meditation is a book by Maureen Garth, entitled *Starbright*, published by Harper Collins. Guided meditation tapes can be found at most large bookstores.

Meditation is an ancient skill which, when practiced regularly, helps clear the mind and restore a sense of peace, tranquility, and general well-being—essential to both the prevention of stress and/or dealing with stress in our lives.

How to get started

To begin, find a quiet, comfortable spot where you will be able to sit, undisturbed for at least fifteen minutes to half an hour. There is no need to sit in any particular position, however, sitting with your back straight will result in less discomfort, especially later on as you lengthen the time you meditate.

If you have a guided meditation tape, this is an excellent way to begin to enjoy the benefits of meditation without the frequent worry many people have of not doing it properly. Once you begin with some guided information to follow, it will be easier later on to meditate in silence comfortably.

If you are beginning without the help of a tape, visualize your thoughts as sentences moving slowly before your eyes. Imagine finding the space in between your thoughts, to focus on, or go between. Here, in this space, there are no thoughts, no words, just space. Try to remain in this space between your thoughts as long as possible. This is much more difficult than it sounds. The constant barrage of thoughts dashing through your mind is quite distracting. You will find that you will need to keep pulling yourself back to the space between your thought. THIS IS NORMAL AND SHOULD BE EXPECTED. Above all don't become impatient with yourself. Just keep gently bringing yourself back and don't get discouraged. With practice, the amount of time that you are able to free your mind of all activity will increase, becoming longer and longer.

The Chinese call the constant barrage of thoughts in our heads the "Chattering Monkeys." Once we've learned to silence the chattering moneys, even for five minutes, we will experience a serenity which will enable us to transcend even the most difficult of life's problems. Most important, you will have taught yourself how to relax your mind, which although it may sound simple—is incredibly healing. Studies have shown that the body's immune system is strengthened with continued meditation. Other studies have shown that experienced meditators are hospitalized far less for ANY reason than those who do not meditate. Unfortunately, not enough people take the time to learn how to rest their minds. Even while we sleep, we dream. Our mind almost never rests. By facilitating rest for our mind, we are doing for our mind, our emotions—our psyche—what sleep does for the body.

By teaching children how to meditate we are giving them the gift of serenity, or perhaps in more popular terms, we are teaching them priceless coping skills, which if practiced, will result in enhanced ability to concentrate, less anxiety, irritation and anger, and more empathy and patience. All of which will enhance individual communication and problem-solving skills, thus promoting better mental health. Again, what you are teaching is a coping skill which will have a lifelong positive impact on the quality of your child's life.

CHAPTER SIXTEEN

Principles of Home Hygiene & Management

In Renaissance times it was thought that sickness and disease were the result of sin, evil influences, night air and other equally unscientific causes. It was not until around the times of Louis Pasteur (Pasteur developed the pasteurization process) that the concept of transmitting germs from person to person was recognized.

Before Pasteur's time, a few observant physicians had noticed a direct cause and effect relationship between the contact of an ill or diseased body and a healthy body. In many instances, the healthy body soon began to develop the same illness the diseased body or object they had been in contact with had developed.

One of the first documented incidents supporting this theory occurred when one of the first physicians who practiced what we now call pathology (the dissection of tissue) observed, that his patients, whom he/she saw after working with corpses, all became ill. he/she surmised this was more than coincidental that only his patients, upon admission to the hospital, became sicker instead of better. This observation prompted the physician to suspect that he/she was possibly responsible for his hospitalized patients decline in health. The physician, began to wash his hands with hot water and soap and change his outer coat after working with the corpses. he/she also thought that it might be helpful to wash between seeing different patients. The results amazed him. His patients health did not decline but improved. The concept of germs was not really understood even then, but the importance of hand washing, especially between patients, was certainly recognized.

Centuries later, in June 1987, a Boston area newspaper *The Tab* ran a special feature on "hospital-acquired" infection. "Hospital-acquired" infection is an infection that the patient contracts while in the hospital because of the transmission of germs from one patient to another. Hospital-acquired infection is believed to be carried from one patient to another by nurses, doctors and other hospital workers, or possibly by dietary (kitchen), laundry, or housekeeping departments due to lack of adherence to hand washing or other "aseptic" (clean techniques). *The Tab* researched and reported that:

- Hospital-acquired infections are believed to be among the nation's 10 leading causes of death killing about 20,000 Americans each year.
- Lack of education in infection prevention is a cause.
- 1985 information on Boston area hospital's showed that one in every 1000 patients who acquires a major infection during hospitalization dies as a result.

Hand Washing Guidelines

Whether you're caring for a young infant, a handicapped child or an older adult, the importance of hand washing cannot be stressed enough. The Nanny will always adhere to the following hygiene and hand washing guidelines.

Germs cannot be seen except with the aid of a microscope. As a result a lay person may not be aware of their existence and may not practice routine hand washing. The Professional Nanny understands the importance of hand washing. Nanny's wash their hands routinely and set an example for children by washing hands thoroughly with soap and warm water in respect to proper health habits.

Nanny's always practice and teach hand washing before preparing meals, after using the toilet, after rendering personal care (especially when dealing with a dressing or wound) and any time after they come in contact with a potentially germ-ridden environment, such as the floor or any soiled article.

The decomposition of food is caused by germs. This is why dishes and pans not washed thoroughly can make a person sick. Food stuck to objects will rot (decompose) if not removed by washing. This also explains why food not properly refrigerated will "go bad". Germs can cause decomposition and if eaten, will make us sick. This is the basis of "food poisoning".

As important as it is to wash our hands, it is equally important to keep the areas we live and work in, clean. Germs are everywhere. Although most will not hurt us, many can and will. If a person has a cold, and coughs and sneezes, although we cannot see the germs go into the air and land on the top of the table or a glass on the kitchen counter, they are there. If someone else without a cold then drinks from the glass on the kitchen counter, the chances are great that that person will also develop a cold.

Areas Most Likely to be Germ Ridden

It is extremely important to keep the environment clean; to protect not only your charges from illness, but yourself as well. Some of the areas most likely to be germ-ridden are:

- The laundry, especially when soiled clothing or bed sheets pile up.
- The bathroom, which should be cleaned daily.

- The kitchen and refrigerator, the kitchen requiring daily cleaning and the refrigerator needing daily checking for any food that has gone "bad."
- Wastebaskets, which are filled with germs and should be emptied before they become full.

Remember that we cannot see germs with the naked eye, so you must protect yourself and your charges from germs by paying special attention to these areas. Wash your hands after coming in contact with any area that may be germ-ridden. Wash your hands before and after giving personal care or preparing food. This practice of washing one's hands and being aware of potential germ ridden areas is referred to as "aseptic technique" in the hospital. As a Nanny you will practice aseptic technique in your every day routine.

HYGIENE POINTS OF EMPHASIS

Kitchen

- Children should be asked and assisted with hand washing before meals.
- Dishes and pans must be thoroughly washed and then checked to be certain all food and/or grease has been removed. This includes sides of pans, inside cover of pan and under handles. Remember decomposed food can make us sick!
- When rinsing dishes and cutler, remove all food particles before placing them in dishwasher, especially when dishwasher is only partially full and not be turned on until it is full or almost full.
- When washing pans do not fill sink and wash "bath-style", instead wash pans "shower style"—keep the hot water running while you thoroughly clean pans and then rinse under water.
- Check pans and other utensils that are not going into dishwasher after washing to be certain all food and grease have been removed.

- After dishes have been washed wiped off around sink and around faucet so that water does not stand. Wash faucet and wipe out sink.
- Counters should be wiped off immediately after preparing meals.
- Food should be put away before the meal or immediately after using.
- Microwave should be wiped out immediately anytime food splatters.
- Use a piece of paper towel to cover food when microwaving to prevent splattering.
- Toasters and toaster ovens should be wiped off daily after use.
- Floor should be swept immediately after meals and mopped if food or liquid spilled during meal.
- Rubbish and garbage removed daily.
- Refrigerator should be checked each week before food shopping to remove old food and to wipe off shelves.
- Stove should be cleaned after each meal.
- Appliance fronts i.e., dishwasher, stove should be checked for any spills and wiped off if necessary.
- High chairs and chairs where children sit should be thoroughly wiped off after each meal.
- Cupboards and cutlery trays should be reorganized whenever necessary.
- A shopping list should be kept on an ongoing basis.
- Clutter should be put in its proper place or in a place where the owner can easily find it to put away.

Bathroom

- Don't leave toys in tub.
- Sink should be cleaned daily with a cleanser and hot water, especially in bathrooms where sinks are used when brushing teeth.
- Clean around faucets and sink.
- Bathtub and/or shower should be cleaned daily.
- Mats in tubs should be removed or turned over and scrubbed.

- Drain should be checked for hair or other debris daily (germs thrive in moist, dark environments) especially before bath time.
- A tablespoon of ammonia should be poured into toilet daily and allowed to sit or 20 minutes or so and then flushed away to prevent bacterial buildup.
- Trash removed daily.
- Never leave a cup in the bathroom for everyone's (or anyone's) use. Use only paper cup dispensers.

FOOD SHOPPING-POINTS OF EMPHASIS

Before shopping, first determine:
A. Inventory of food present in the house.
B. List prepared food from menu and number of servings needed.
  1. Canned or frozen foods can be purchased monthly provided there is a place to store them.
  2. Fresh vegetables, fruits and dairy products should not be purchased more than a week from the time they are to be consumed. Otherwise they may spoil.
  3. Always read the labels on food packages for amount of servings and ingredients which may be restricted.
  4. When reading ingredients in any packaged food, keep in mind that the ingredient present in the greatest amount will be listed first and so on.
  5. Use coupons to purchase products whenever possible unless your employer objects.
  6. Purchase products on "special" or store brand products which are less expensive.
  7. Store foods and other products according to directions on package.

8.   Always look for expiration date on perishable foods and be cer-
     tain they will be used before the expiration date stamped on the
     package.
9.   After opening perishable products, be certain they are closed or
     covered properly. They will maintain their freshness longer,
     taste better and you will save money in the long run.
10. Mark the date on the container of all leftovers placed into
     refrigerator.

C. If your employer is not accompanying you to the store,
    1.   Document the amount of money he/she/he/she has given you
         and always save the receipt, for your employer's records.

You should not purchase items for yourself with your employer's
order. Instead separate the employer's order from yours and keep the
receipts and the change separate. This will avoid possible confusion and
misunderstandings.

The Master Shopping List

A master shopping list is a great tool which when utilized will virtually
eliminate the chances of "forgetting" one item or another at the store.
You should first list one category, add all the items you generally buy in
that category and go on to the next, including quantities.

The best way to help you remember all items in each category is to
first plant he/she weekly menu including all meals and snacks (see
Nutrition). then think through each meal listing the necessary ingredients and amounts according to servings. The general categories on the
following example. are in order you will most likely find them in large
supermarkets.

After devising your own Master List, have it typed and copied (about 20
copies should do.) Keep a copy on the refrigerator or in a conspicuous

place where you can easily check things off as you notice they are needed. Before shopping, use the Master List to check grocery inventory. Check off anything that's needed and post another copy of the refrigerator for the following week.

STERILIZING & PREPARING BABY'S BOTTLES

Babies are especially vulnerable to germs and therefore it is essential that procedures be strictly followed when it comes to preparing bottles. Once the infant is two months old or so, you can use aseptic technique instead of sterilizing.

Procedure for Sterilizing Bottles

1. Wash your hands thoroughly
2. Using a separate basin, wash all bottles, can opener, nipples, collars and equipment used in preparation.
3. Take each nipple and hold under hot water and soap. Put your thumb over largest part and squeeze hot soapy water through small nipple; hold until water runs clear and all soap is removed.
4. Wash all edges of nipple, rinse thoroughly.
5. Wash inside collar, rinse thoroughly.
6. Put collar and nipple together.
7. Store in sterilized strainer or other container.
8. Use a bottle brush to clean bottles.
9. Wash around top where nipple screws on.
10. Place bottles, tongs, etc. into a sterilizer or large pan.
11. Add a few, 2-3 inches, of water.
12. Boil.
13. Put lid on and leave it on while water boils for 7 minutes.
14. Allow to cool.
15. Place upside down on clean surface.

Procedure for Opening Formula Can

- Clean top of can with hot water and soap.
- Dry off.
- Use sterilized can opener to open.

Procedure for Filling and Storing Sterilized Bottles

- Turn bottles over (you can touch the outside).
- Fill each bottle with the same amount of formula.
- Wash your hands thoroughly.
- Place inverted (nipple facing down) nipple assembly on bottle.
- Store in refrigerator.
- All must be used or discarded with in 48 hours.

Before Feeding

- Heat formula in bottle.
- Shake to mix hot and cold spots of formula to avoid burning babies mouth.
- Shake a few drops on arm, if neither hot nor cold, then feed.

About the Author

Anne Merchant is uniquely fitted to write this book. After finishing her nurse training at Massachusetts General Hospital, she founded Primary Nursing, Inc. A Home Health Care Corporation, and Professional Nanny, Inc., a nanny placement & training service in Wellesley, MA. She has written training curriculums which have been offered at the college level, including the first expanded Home Health/Child Development curriculum approved by the Massachusetts Department of Public Health, Division of Health Care Quality. For nannies who could not attend school full time, she developed the first Weekend Associate Degree Program for nannies in conjunction with Wheelock College in Boston, MA.

She developed the first tuition-free distance nanny training and in-service program which currently enrolls nannies worldwide. She is a past executive committee member of the International Nanny Association and also served as Treasurer for the INA for two years. She currently writes monthly advice columns for nanny & parenting publications and websites. She has been a guest speaker at colleges and on television and radio talk shows internationally.

Index

A

Accidents, 90, 92, 103, 140, 160, 162, 234

Acne, 154, 210

Abdominal tenderness, 148

Abuse, 12, 17, 76, 140, 174

Active Listening, 54, 125

Activity, 16, 25-26, 32-33, 52, 67, 69-70, 120, 130, 132, 135, 166, 209-211, 214, 238, 240

Adolescence, 112, 180, 232

Adulthood, 113, 232

Airbag, 104

Alcoholism, 237

Allergies, 154, 189, 227

Anger, 10, 71, 75, 80, 123, 163-164, 168, 171, 234, 241

Anxiety, 7, 18, 58-59, 71, 75, 80, 138, 147, 203, 233-234, 236, 241

Antibiotic, 210-211, 228

Appendicitis, 216

Appendixes, 216

Appetite, 66-67, 134, 187-188, 190-191

Appliances, 49, 84, 86-88, 91, 94, 99

Aspirin, 209, 216-217, 222

Assertion, 58

Asthma*****

Aseptic technique, 52-53, 245, 249

Attitude, 20-21, 57-58, 60-63, 116, 118, 133, 135, 148, 161-162, 192

    Inquiring, 61

Professional, 1, 5-6, 8, 19-23, 27-31, 37, 52, 60, 62, 75, 128, 164, 166-167, 170, 174, 218, 244, 251
    Relaxed, 52, 55, 148, 160, 162, 203
    Therapeutic, 60
At-Home Parent, 13
Authenticity, 126, 235-236
Automobile, 9, 93
Autonomy, 108
Awareness skills, 56

B
Baby, 7, 23, 33-34, 40-41, 46, 63, 90-91, 93-94, 123, 138-139, 146-158, 171, 174-175, 186-190, 192-193, 195-204, 210, 249
    Bottle, 33, 44, 49, 67, 71, 158, 186-188, 203, 210, 249-250
    Seat, 49, 93, 104, 150
    Talk, 9, 11, 14, 18, 26, 34, 44, 54, 56, 61, 63-65, 72, 78-79, 121-124, 129-131, 133-135, 157, 161, 169, 171, 175, 188, 192, 233-234, 238, 251
    Teeth, 32, 42, 49, 70, 155, 157, 182, 194, 203-205, 246
Bathing, 22, 32, 40-42, 88, 94, 146, 153, 195, 197, 205-206
Bathroom, 23, 35, 39-41, 46, 48-49, 70, 87-88, 92, 94, 124, 159, 161-162, 205, 216, 224, 244, 246-247
Bedroom, 23, 35, 48, 88, 100, 158
Benefits, 4, 24, 28, 239-240
Blood level, 223
Board of Health, 92, 219
Bonus, 11
Bottle, 33, 44, 49, 67, 71, 158, 186-188, 203, 210, 249-250
Bowel movement, 68
Breakfast, 32, 35, 37, 42, 69
Breast, 26, 146-150, 156-157, 186, 188
    Feeding, 22, 32, 94, 147-150, 156-158, 186-189, 192, 202, 250
    Milk, 26, 39, 156-157, 180, 182, 185-186, 188-189, 191, 194, 203, 209, 224

Pump, 186
Tenderness, 147-148
Brush teeth, 32
Bulb syringe, 152
Burns, 94, 99, 103, 211
Buckets, 87, 103
Burping, 149, 187

C
Cabinet locks, 92
Caesarean recovery, 148
Car seat, 93
Certified, 19
Chattering Monkeys, 240
Chickenpox, 215
Child Development, 81, 109, 134, 164, 251
Childproof, 84, 170-171
Children's, 23-24, 27, 33, 36, 49, 52-53, 64, 67, 77, 84-85, 95, 100, 129, 132-133, 141, 159, 161, 168, 207
    Bathroom, 23, 35, 39-41, 46, 48-49, 70, 87-88, 92, 94, 124, 159, 161-162, 205, 216, 224, 244, 246-247
    Bedroom, 23, 35, 48, 88, 100, 158
    Clothes, 24, 44, 49-50, 98, 124, 201-202, 206, 210
    Equipment, 23, 36, 42, 53, 91, 95, 195, 197, 200, 205, 249
Choking, 40, 89, 94, 103, 203
Choices, 65, 86, 118, 193-194
Choosing toys, 139, 141
Chores, 14, 33
Circumcision, 152, 197
Cleaners, 103
Cognitive, 29, 70-71, 134
Cold wars, 16

Cold, 16, 50, 94, 107, 139, 148, 161, 196, 198, 201, 205, 207, 210, 212, 214, 216, 222, 228, 244, 250

Colic, 156

Comfort, 120, 129, 148, 150, 153, 156, 188-189, 202, 209, 213

Common Illness*****

Communication, 5, 7-8, 10, 16, 20, 54-60, 62-63, 65, 72, 122, 124-126, 223, 235, 241

    Children, 4-7, 9-10, 13, 16-19, 21-25, 27-30, 32-33, 36, 38, 40-41, 43-46, 49-50, 52-55, 60, 63-68, 71, 73, 77-80, 83-85, 92-95, 97-100, 103, 108-111, 114, 117-120, 123-126, 128-134, 136-141, 147-148, 155, 159-162, 164, 166, 168-169, 171-175, 180-183, 185, 189-194, 199, 202, 204-209, 212-214, 216-217, 219-221, 229, 235-236, 238-239, 241, 244-246

    Non-verbal, 55, 58, 64

    Parents, 4-5, 8, 10-11, 13, 16-19, 21-24, 39, 43, 55, 57, 60, 63-67, 74, 78-80, 84, 90-91, 100, 111, 114, 116, 119, 128, 131, 133, 136-137, 139, 146, 153, 158, 164, 168, 170-171, 174, 188-189, 200-203, 206, 208, 211, 214, 223, 228, 237

    Scripts, 57

    Tips, 124-125, 200

    Verbal, 17, 58, 122-123, 163, 192

    Written, 11, 20, 28-30, 65, 147, 172, 220, 229, 251

Community resources, 22

Compatibility*****

Competence, 110-112

Condiments, 182, 194

Confidentiality, 77

Conflicts, 12, 234

Congestion, 148, 151, 212

Consistency, 13, 29, 151, 157, 167, 170

Constipation, 150-151

Continuity of care, 29, 66

Contract, 4, 20, 24
Coordination, 70, 134, 224
Coping, 16, 117, 174, 229, 236, 239, 241
Corner guards, 92
CPR, 6
Cradle cap, 156
Crossed eyes, 155
Croup, 216
Crying, 71, 146, 149-150, 156-157, 174, 188
Curfew, 8, 73
Curiosity, 83-84, 108, 165, 170
Curriculum, 22-23, 31, 128, 130, 134, 251
Cutting teeth, 157

D
Daily Log, 5-6, 23, 30, 65, 67-69, 191, 223
Danger signals, 218
Death, 99, 103, 117, 229-230, 234, 237, 243
Decomposition, 244
Dental, 96, 181, 203, 207, 226
    Care, 3, 7, 17-18, 21-23, 25-27, 29, 31-32, 37, 42, 52, 66, 74, 77-80, 96, 107, 110, 116, 118-119, 123, 128, 134-135, 137, 140, 146, 148, 152-153, 157, 164, 166-167, 169-170, 173-174, 177, 181-182, 186, 190, 192, 197-198, 200, 202, 204-208, 210, 215, 217-218, 223, 226-227, 229, 239, 244-245, 251
    Disease, 179, 185-186, 203, 213, 215, 242
    Hygiene, 22-23, 27, 31-32, 35, 48-49, 70, 147, 153, 195, 202-205, 207, 211, 242-243, 245
Dentist, 96, 181, 203-204, 226-227
Depression, 146-147, 213, 231, 234

Development, 6, 16, 19, 29, 52, 65, 67, 70, 81, 84-85, 100, 106-115, 117-118, 120, 122, 130, 133-135, 137-138, 141, 163-166, 173, 179-181, 191-192, 194, 213, 217, 232, 251
    Cognitive, 29, 70-71, 134
    Physical, 17, 52, 55, 69-70, 113, 117, 134, 140, 146, 171, 173-174, 179-180, 229, 234, 239
    Psychological, 70-71, 79, 106, 134-135
    Social, 12, 29, 52, 56, 70-71, 77, 85, 111-112, 114, 116-117, 134-137, 173-174, 192, 217, 229-230, 234
    Spiritual, 229, 234
Diabetes, 185, 211
Diarrhea, 151, 154, 221
Diaper, 70, 151-152, 154, 160-162, 196-199, 210, 221
    Area, 18-19, 23, 27, 32, 65, 84, 86, 99, 153-154, 156, 196-199, 205, 210, 243, 245
    Change, 8, 14, 30, 32-33, 36, 42, 44, 50, 62, 97, 137, 141, 147, 149-152, 154, 156, 158, 164, 167, 198-199, 202, 212-213, 230-235, 243, 248
    Rash, 41, 70, 153-154, 198-199, 208-209, 214-215
Digital, 219-220
Dinner, 8, 12, 35, 66-67, 69, 79, 155, 158, 171
Discharge, 152, 155
Discipline, 13-14, 165
Dishes, 23, 35, 48, 110, 190, 244-246
Diversion, 166, 170-171
Divorce, 229, 237
Dose, 224, 235
Dosing spoon, 228
Dressing, 22, 32, 44, 200-201, 206, 244
Drowning, 94, 103
Dynamic, 3, 11, 13, 74-76, 235

E

Ear infection, 209

Eating Habits, 65, 179, 191, 231, 234

EDITH, 98

Education, 19, 83, 85, 133, 188, 243

Educational Play, 133

Elimination, 67, 70

Emergencies, 6

Emotional, 29, 52, 61-62, 76, 112-113, 117-119, 134, 179-180, 229, 234, 236
   Connection, 112, 119, 124, 231
      Health, 49, 89, 92, 116-117, 134, 140, 177, 179-182, 185-186, 190, 203, 208, 219, 227, 230, 236, 239, 241-244, 251

Empathy, 7, 60-61, 112, 124, 241

Engorgement, 147

Epidemic, 210

Epilepsy, 214

Eriksson*****

Errands, 7, 12, 24

Erythema Toxicum, 153

Escape Drills In The Home, 98

Ethical Dynamic, 74-76

Evaluation, 28-29, 52

Exercise, 6-8, 63, 67, 69, 72, 109, 134, 211, 233-234

Expanders, 61

Expiration date, 247-248

Extrovert, 121

F

Falls, 46, 84, 91-92, 95, 187, 197, 199, 211, 224

Family activities, 24

Fatigue, 147, 151, 212-213, 232, 234

Feeding, 22, 32, 94, 147-150, 156-158, 186-189, 192, 202, 250
    Blister, 156
    On demand, 186
Fidelity, 112-113
Fire, 90, 97-100
    Drill, 97, 99
    Escape, 98
    Exit, 98-100
    Extinguisher, 97, 100
    Hazard, 6, 8, 91, 140
    Ladders, 98-99
    Safety, 6, 8, 21, 86, 90, 92-93, 97-98, 100, 103-105, 139-140
    Station, 99-100
First aid, 6, 228
    Form, 6, 10, 13, 28, 69, 111-112, 116, 146-147, 151, 163, 166, 168, 182, 189, 209, 227
    Supplies, 35
Floor, 15, 23, 35, 41, 43-45, 47-50, 88, 90-92, 95, 98-99, 124, 140, 161, 164, 168, 244, 246
Flu, 212
Fluids, 140, 148, 161-162, 191, 210, 212-213, 222
Fluoride, 181, 205
Fontanel, 156
Food, 15, 22, 24, 38, 40, 48-49, 94, 149, 154, 166, 169, 171, 179-183, 185-186, 188-193, 211, 224, 244-247
    Attitudes, 22, 58, 133, 192
    Likes And Dislikes, 190
    Shopping, 32, 36, 45, 130, 147, 246-249
Formula, 26, 149-150, 156-157, 187-189, 203, 250
Friend, 15, 56, 60, 75, 230, 233, 237
Friends & Visits, 14, 112
Fuse Box, 97

G
Germ Ridden, 244-245
German measles, 215
Germs, 207, 242-245, 247, 249
Good behavior, 170, 172
Gradual transition, 18
Grooming, 32, 42, 202
Growth & Development, 6, 19, 52, 67, 70, 106, 113, 118, 120, 180, 191
Guilt, 64, 109, 167, 169, 171, 234

H
Hair, 32-33, 41-42, 52, 70, 155, 202, 205, 207, 227, 247
Hair loss, 155
Hand Washing, 211, 243-245
Hearing tests, 217
Hazard, 6, 8, 91, 140
Heat, 99, 154, 201, 210, 250
    Rash, 41, 70, 153-154, 198-199, 208-209, 214-215
    Stroke, 185, 210
Heimlich, 94
Helmets, 103
Hemorrhoids, 148
High self-esteem, 61, 118-119, 122, 239
Home, 3, 5-8, 13-15, 20, 22-23, 25-27, 29, 31-32, 35, 43, 45, 48, 53, 66, 72, 74, 77, 79, 84-85, 91-93, 95, 97-100, 104, 133, 137, 147, 156, 158, 165, 173-175, 177, 182, 195, 210, 219, 230-232, 242, 251
    Management, 22, 27, 29, 31-32, 35, 48, 53, 119, 147, 165, 242
    Safety, 6, 8, 21, 86, 90, 92-93, 97-98, 100, 103-105, 139-140
    Security, 67, 95, 109, 116-117
Hospital-acquired infection, 243
Hotline, 77
Household tension, 237

Housework, 15, 24, 34, 49

Humidifier, 216

Hygiene, 22-23, 27, 31-32, 35, 48-49, 70, 147, 153, 195, 202-205, 207, 211, 242-243, 245

Habits, 8, 11, 22, 65, 77, 158, 160-161, 179, 181-182, 187, 191-193, 205, 230-231, 234, 244

Home, 3, 5-8, 13-15, 20, 22-23, 25-27, 29, 31-32, 35, 43, 45, 48, 53, 66, 72, 74, 77, 79, 84-85, 91-93, 95, 97-100, 104, 133, 137, 147, 156, 158, 165, 173-175, 177, 182, 195, 210, 219, 230-232, 242, 251

Hygiene, 22-23, 27, 31-32, 35, 48-49, 70, 147, 153, 195, 202-205, 207, 211, 242-243, 245

Management, 22, 27, 29, 31-32, 35, 48, 53, 119, 147, 165, 242

I

I Statements, 61

Identity, 95, 110-113

Identity confusion, 112

Illness, 208-209, 211-212, 215-216, 230, 237, 242, 244

Immunization, 212, 214-215

Impetigo contagiosa, 210

Impulse control, 163, 172

Inappropriate, 23, 79-80, 86, 89, 238

Incubation Period, 209-215

Infant, 17, 23, 30, 70-71, 94-95, 107-108, 138-140, 149-151, 154-158, 186-190, 192, 195-196, 200-201, 203, 209-210, 215-216, 228, 243, 249

Infection, 152-154, 199, 205, 209, 212, 215-216, 220, 243

Ear, 197, 209

Prevention, 100, 185-186, 205, 239, 243

Infectious keratoconjunctivitis, 211

Infectious mononucleosis, 213

Influenza, 212-213

Initiative, 109-110

Insect Bites, 206
Intellectual, 61, 75, 229, 235
Internet, 16, 19
Interpersonal problem solving, 62
Interview, 4, 13
Intestinal Gas, 148
Introverts, 121
Iron, 36, 181, 193
IRS mileage allowance, 9
Isolation, 113, 208-210, 212-215

J
Job, 3, 6-8, 12-15, 17-20, 25, 28, 47, 59, 92, 119, 125, 146, 190, 231-232, 234
    Satisfaction, 24-25, 118-119, 130
    Offer, 9-10, 13, 19, 38, 140, 149-150, 161, 182, 186
Judgmental, 17, 34, 79, 122

K
Keeping the Daily Log, 67
Kitchen, 5, 15, 23, 32, 35, 40-42, 44-50, 65, 78, 85-87, 92, 134, 161, 243-245

L
Language, 21, 56, 64, 68, 131, 163, 165, 217
Laundry, 23, 35-36, 44, 47, 49-50, 88, 139, 147, 243-244
Laxative, 148
Lead paint detector, 92
Learning, 19, 62, 71, 83-86, 111-112, 119-121, 125, 128, 133, 137, 160, 163, 217, 232
    Styles, 119-120, 122
Leaving, 11, 18, 47, 76, 206, 230, 232, 235
Lethargy, 215
Library, 26, 32-34, 47

Limits, 8, 13, 72, 86, 88, 110, 130, 165-170, 211
Liquids, 69, 86, 94, 182, 203, 224
Louis Pasteur, 242
Low Fat, 180
Lunch, 15, 33, 35, 37, 48, 66-67, 69, 193
Lunch box, 193

M
Maid, 15, 206
Managing Stress, 229, 233
Master Shopping List, 248
Meal planning, 22, 35, 190
Meal preparation, 35
Measles, 214-215
Medical information, 5-6
Medication, 154, 157, 206, 209, 211, 214, 223-224
Meditation, 238-240
Meeting Place, 98, 100
Menu, 24, 37-38, 190, 192, 247-248
Mercury thermometer, 219-220
Middle-age, 57
Microwave, 38, 94, 246
Monilia, 154
Moodiness, 21
Moral character, 21
Mother, 7, 79, 96, 146-151, 164, 186, 215, 218, 226
Move, 41, 106, 113, 116, 159, 169, 204, 214, 231, 237
Music, 33-34, 138, 171, 234
    Lessons, 22, 33-34, 98, 137
    Listening, 33, 54-56, 119, 124-125

N

Nail, 22, 200, 206

    Care, 3, 7, 17-18, 21-23, 25-27, 29, 31-32, 37, 42, 52, 66, 74, 77-80, 96, 107, 110, 116, 118-119, 123, 128, 134-135, 137, 140, 146, 148, 152-153, 157, 164, 166-167, 169-170, 173-174, 177, 181-182, 186, 190, 192, 197-198, 200, 202, 204-208, 210, 215, 217-218, 223, 226-227, 229, 239, 244-245, 251

    Clipper, 200

Name-calling, 135

Nanny, 3-22, 24, 26-34, 36-38, 40, 42, 44, 46, 48, 50, 52, 55-56, 58-60, 62-66, 68-72, 76-80, 84-86, 88, 90, 92, 94, 96, 98, 100, 104, 106-108, 110-112, 114, 116, 119-120, 122, 124-126, 128, 130-140, 142, 144, 148, 150, 152, 154, 156, 158, 160, 162, 164, 166, 168, 170, 172, 174, 179-180, 182, 184, 186, 188, 190, 192, 194, 196, 198, 200, 202, 204, 206, 210, 212, 214, 216, 218, 220, 222-224, 226-230, 232, 234-238, 240, 243-246, 248, 250-251, 254, 256, 258, 260, 262, 264, 266

Nap, 33, 43, 53, 65-67, 158, 162

Network, 19

New, 4-8, 16, 26, 30, 52, 68, 71, 90, 117, 120, 130, 134, 138, 146-147, 158, 161, 165, 171, 183, 185, 189, 199, 212, 230-232, 234-235, 237

    Mother, 7, 79, 96, 146-151, 164, 186, 215, 218, 226

    Nanny, 3-22, 24, 26-34, 36-38, 40, 42, 44, 46, 48, 50, 52, 55-56, 58-60, 62-66, 68-72, 76-80, 84-86, 88, 90, 92, 94, 96, 98, 100, 104, 106-108, 110-112, 114, 116, 119-120, 122, 124-126, 128, 130-140, 142, 144, 148, 150, 152, 154, 156, 158, 160, 162, 164, 166, 168, 170, 172, 174, 179-180, 182, 184, 186, 188, 190, 192, 194, 196, 198, 200, 202, 204, 206, 210, 212, 214, 216, 218, 220, 222-224, 226-230, 232, 234-238, 240, 243-246, 248, 250-251, 254, 256, 258, 260, 262, 264, 266

    Position, 4-5, 7, 12-13, 19, 22, 24, 29-30, 32, 59, 93, 146, 150, 155, 174, 198, 239

    School, 3, 22, 24, 34, 38, 42, 44, 48, 71, 79, 110-111, 118, 130, 136, 138, 142-145, 185, 193-194, 204, 212, 217, 230, 235, 237, 239, 251

    Teacher, 79, 128, 237

Newborn, 26, 146, 152, 154, 158, 173, 210
    Acne, 154, 210
    Care, 3, 7, 17-18, 21-23, 25-27, 29, 31-32, 37, 42, 52, 66, 74, 77-80,
    96, 107, 110, 116, 118-119, 123, 128, 134-135, 137, 140, 146, 148,
    152-153, 157, 164, 166-167, 169-170, 173-174, 177, 181-182, 186,
    190, 192, 197-198, 200, 202, 204-208, 210, 215, 217-218, 223, 226-
    227, 229, 239, 244-245, 251
    Sleep routine, 158
Nipple, 148, 156, 249-250
Non-skid strips, 92
Normal Body Temperature, 220
Nursery rhyme, 45-47
Nutrition, 37, 69, 179, 183, 185, 193, 248

O
Obstacles to, 59, 169
    Healthy Communication, 59
    Setting Limits, 165, 168, 170
Obstetrician, 148
Old Age, 114-117
Older Children, 23, 36, 95, 134, 140, 147-148, 159-161, 175, 182, 189,
191, 202, 205-206
On duty, 9, 12, 14, 21, 24, 26
On Time, 10, 223
One-year minimum, 11
Outlet covers, 92
Oral, 213, 220, 222
Organizing, 22, 27, 130, 167
    Your Time, 27, 170, 175
    Environment, 5, 13, 16, 19, 23, 53, 57, 61, 85, 90, 107-108, 120, 122-
    123, 147, 163, 165-167, 170, 173, 212, 219, 234, 238, 244

Orientation, 5-6, 8, 133
   Assignments, 6
   To family, 5, 8
Overtired, 150

P
Pacifier, 43-44, 50, 94, 149-150, 158, 203
Parent, 3-4, 6, 11, 13-15, 17, 22, 29, 45, 65-66, 69, 74, 107, 110-111, 133, 164, 171, 190, 220, 223, 227, 235-237
   Laid off, 237
   Travels, 237
   Illness, 208-209, 211-212, 215-216, 230, 237, 242, 244
   Directives, 17
   Guidelines, 4, 17, 23, 39, 44, 46, 63, 72, 130, 135, 140, 175, 185, 189, 201, 205, 243
   Separate, 11, 13, 15, 24, 36, 109, 111, 160, 237, 248-249
Pediatric, 5-6, 203, 208, 218
   Illness, 208-209, 211-212, 215-216, 230, 237, 242, 244
   Medication, 154, 157, 206, 209, 211, 214, 223-224
Pediatrician, 96, 147, 149-157, 181, 188-189, 191, 199, 206, 208-209, 212, 216, 220-223, 226-227
Perfectionism*****
Personal, 9, 20-22, 25, 27, 31-32, 37, 61, 63, 72, 74-75, 77, 109-111, 113, 121, 153, 188, 230, 233, 244-245
   Care, 3, 7, 17-18, 21-23, 25-27, 29, 31-32, 37, 42, 52, 66, 74, 77-80, 96, 107, 110, 116, 118-119, 123, 128, 134-135, 137, 140, 146, 148, 152-153, 157, 164, 166-167, 169-170, 173-174, 177, 181-182, 186, 190, 192, 197-198, 200, 202, 204-208, 210, 215, 217-218, 223, 226-227, 229, 239, 244-245, 251
   Problems, 4, 16-17, 21, 54-55, 60, 62, 75, 85, 116-118, 125, 182, 208, 233, 235, 240

Pet, 8, 32, 48, 212, 237
    Dies, 237, 243
    Ill, 12, 164, 208-209, 237, 242
Pharmacist, 223-224
Philosophies, 17
Physical, 17, 52, 55, 69-70, 113, 117, 134, 140, 146, 171, 173-174, 179-180, 229, 234, 239
Play, 6, 22-23, 32-34, 41, 43, 45-48, 52-53, 65, 67, 74, 87-88, 93-95, 106, 109-110, 120, 122-123, 127-138, 141, 147, 157, 165-166, 168-170, 172, 202, 212
    Creative, 6, 17, 23, 53-54, 126, 128-130, 133, 147-148, 165-166, 169-170, 181
    Playgroup, 5, 33, 45-46, 67, 79, 136
    Play Plan, 22, 46-47, 134, 138, 172
    Structured, 32-33, 52, 130-131
    Unstructured, 32-33, 44, 52-53, 67, 130-132
    Infant Play Plan, 138
Plants, 84, 90-91
Poison, 96, 104, 206, 226, 228
    Control, 76, 83, 88, 96-97, 139, 160, 163-166, 168, 170-172, 193, 213-214, 226, 233-234
    Ivy, 206, 228
    Oak, 44, 206
Pollyanna, 25
Portfolio, 12
Positive, 22, 55, 60-63, 80, 110, 114-115, 118, 120, 123-125, 133, 135, 138, 160, 165, 167, 171, 175, 231, 241
    Self-esteem, 19, 25, 61-62, 64, 110, 118-120, 122, 124-126, 133, 135, 160, 166, 239
    Stress, 6, 34, 80, 138, 140, 147, 162, 170-171, 180, 229, 231-237, 239
Potty, 32-33, 40, 42, 67-68, 70, 159-163
    Chair, 46-47, 49-50, 161, 204
    Training Outline, Plan, 160

Powder, 39, 41, 198-199
Power struggles, 64, 166, 170
Praise, 111, 125-127, 131, 135, 160-161, 170
    Evaluative, 125-127, 131
    Non-evaluative, 111, 125, 127, 131, 135
Pregnant, 185, 215
Prejudice, 57, 158
Preschooler, 13, 109, 134, 163
Pre-verbal, 18, 71, 80, 131
Privacy, 7-8, 20, 72, 205, 221
Process, 5, 7-8, 10, 27-31, 37, 52, 56-57, 62-63, 71-72, 75, 77, 98, 108, 115-117, 126, 128-130, 161-162, 164, 170, 232, 242
    Recording, 7-8, 10, 71-72
    Forms, 4-5, 58
Professional, 0-1, 5-6, 8, 19-23, 27-31, 37, 52, 60, 62, 75, 128, 164, 166-167, 170, 174, 218, 244, 251
    Attitude, 20-21, 57-58, 60-63, 116, 118, 133, 135, 148, 161-162, 192
    Development, 6, 16, 19, 29, 52, 65, 67, 70, 81, 84-85, 100, 106-115, 117-118, 120, 122, 130, 133-135, 137-138, 141, 163-166, 173, 179-181, 191-192, 194, 213, 217, 232, 251
    Nanny, 3-22, 24, 26-34, 36-38, 40, 42, 44, 46, 48, 50, 52, 55-56, 58-60, 62-66, 68-72, 76-80, 84-86, 88, 90, 92, 94, 96, 98, 100, 104, 106-108, 110-112, 114, 116, 119-120, 122, 124-126, 128, 130-140, 142, 144, 148, 150, 152, 154, 156, 158, 160, 162, 164, 166, 168, 170, 172, 174, 179-180, 182, 184, 186, 188, 190, 192, 194, 196, 198, 200, 202, 204, 206, 210, 212, 214, 216, 218, 220, 222-224, 226-230, 232, 234-238, 240, 243-246, 248, 250-251, 254, 256, 258, 260, 262, 264, 266
    Nanny Online, 5-6, 8, 19
    Nanny process, 27-31, 37, 52
Projectile, 93
Proper Toothbrush, 204
Protein, 179, 183, 194

Psychological, 70-71, 79, 106, 134-135
    Development, 6, 16, 19, 29, 52, 65, 67, 70, 81, 84-85, 100, 106-115,
    117-118, 120, 122, 130, 133-135, 137-138, 141, 163-166, 173, 179-
    181, 191-192, 194, 213, 217, 232, 251

Q
Q-tips, 42, 197
Quiet-time*****
Quivers, 156

R
Range, 183, 208-210, 213, 215-216
Reading stories, 33
Receipt, 248
Recognizing Stress, 232
Rectal, 219-221, 228
References, 4, 13
Regress*****
Relationship maintenance, 9-10
Religious customs, 24
Reporting to the Physician, 220
Research Project Workbooks, 4
Resentment, 10, 15
Review, 6-7, 11, 72, 125, 131
Reyes syndrome, 209, 215-217
Ritualistic, 30
Rivalry, 147, 172-173, 175
Role, 9, 16, 20-22, 24, 56, 58, 73, 106, 112, 114, 122, 128, 130, 165, 180,
185-186, 188
Role model, 21-22, 73, 165
Room temperature, 196
Roseola, 209

Routine, 5, 7, 13, 29-30, 40, 43, 52, 121, 128, 134, 153, 158, 160, 200, 205-206, 220, 244-245
RPW, 4

S
Safety, 6, 8, 21, 86, 90, 92-93, 97-98, 100, 103-105, 139-140
    Assessment, 5-6, 29, 63
    Automobile, 9, 93
    Checklist, 31, 104, 205, 228
    Commission, 103-104, 140
    Fire, 90, 97-100
    Home, 3, 5-8, 13-15, 20, 22-23, 25-27, 29, 31-32, 35, 43, 45, 48, 53,
        66, 72, 74, 77, 79, 84-85, 91-93, 95, 97-100, 104, 133, 137, 147, 156,
        158, 165, 173-175, 177, 182, 195, 210, 219, 230-232, 242, 251
    Playground, 48, 69
    Seat, 49, 93, 104, 150
    Social, 12, 29, 52, 56, 70-71, 77, 85, 111-112, 114, 116-117, 134-137,
        173-174, 192, 217, 229-230, 234
    Statistics, 103
    Tips, 124-125, 200
    Traffic, 104-105
    Water, 35, 39-42, 50, 87-88, 94, 97, 103, 130, 150, 152, 154, 181-182,
        191, 195-197, 205, 210, 216, 221-222, 243-246, 249-250
Salary, 4, 9, 11-12, 15, 19, 24, 72
    Increases, 11, 19, 134, 188, 231
Salt, 39-40, 182
Scabies, 212
Scarlet fever, 213
Schedule, 12, 14, 17, 24, 29, 52, 158, 161-162, 170, 186, 190
School, 3, 22, 24, 34, 38, 42, 44, 48, 71, 79, 110-111, 118, 130, 136, 138,
    142-145, 185, 193-194, 204, 212, 217, 230, 235, 237, 239, 251
School-age, 22-23, 112, 130

Security, 67, 95, 109, 116-117
Self-, 3, 23, 59, 110, 117, 120, 122, 164, 167-168, 171, 234
    Awareness, 56
    Control, 76, 83, 88, 96-97, 139, 160, 163-166, 168, 170-172, 193, 213-214, 226, 233-234
    Esteem, 123, 125, 167-168, 171, 234
Setting limits, 165, 168, 170
Sexual, 17, 234
Shopping list, 36, 130, 246, 248
Sibling, 132, 147, 172-175, 192, 237
Sibling rivalry, 147, 172-173, 175
Side effects, 223
Significant other, 14
Skateboard, 103
Skin, 41-42, 138, 154, 196-199, 201, 205-206, 210, 212, 215
    Burn, 41, 211
    Care, 3, 7, 17-18, 21-23, 25-27, 29, 31-32, 37, 42, 52, 66, 74, 77-80, 96, 107, 110, 116, 118-119, 123, 128, 134-135, 137, 140, 146, 148, 152-153, 157, 164, 166-167, 169-170, 173-174, 177, 181-182, 186, 190, 192, 197-198, 200, 202, 204-208, 210, 215, 217-218, 223, 226-227, 229, 239, 244-245, 251
Sleep, 8, 43-44, 66, 69, 73, 134, 150-151, 157-158, 186, 190, 232, 234, 240
    Patterns, 157-158, 167, 171, 192, 234
    Routine, 5, 7, 13, 29-30, 40, 43, 52, 121, 128, 134, 153, 158, 160, 200, 205-206, 220, 244-245
Smoke Detectors, 97, 100
Smothering, 94, 108
Social, 12, 29, 52, 56, 70-71, 77, 85, 111-112, 114, 116-117, 134-137, 173-174, 192, 217, 229-230, 234
    Development, 6, 16, 19, 29, 52, 65, 67, 70, 81, 84-85, 100, 106-115, 117-118, 120, 122, 130, 133-135, 137-138, 141, 163-166, 173, 179-181, 191-192, 194, 213, 217, 232, 251
    Safety, 6, 8, 21, 86, 90, 92-93, 97-98, 100, 103-105, 139-140

Society, 18, 74-76, 109, 116-117, 119
Soft spot, 156
Solid foods, 188
Sore throat, 212-213
Spiritual, 229, 234
Spoon Feeding, 189
Strep throat, 213
Sterilizing Bottles, 249
Stop, drop and roll, 98
Stress, 6, 34, 80, 138, 140, 147, 162, 170-171, 180, 229, 231-237, 239
    Children, 4-7, 9-10, 13, 16-19, 21-25, 27-30, 32-33, 36, 38, 40-41, 43-46, 49-50, 52-55, 60, 63-68, 71, 73, 77-80, 83-85, 92-95, 97-100, 103, 108-111, 114, 117-120, 123-126, 128-134, 136-141, 147-148, 155, 159-162, 164, 166, 168-169, 171-175, 180-183, 185, 189-194, 199, 202, 204-209, 212-214, 216-217, 219-221, 229, 235-236, 238-239, 241, 244-246
    Environment, 5, 13, 16, 19, 23, 53, 57, 61, 85, 90, 107-108, 120, 122-123, 147, 163, 165-167, 170, 173, 212, 219, 234, 238, 244
    Recognizing, 62, 232
    Stressor, 231
Suckle, 149
Suction, 152, 202
Sugar, 39, 179-182, 211
Sun Exposure, 206
Suppositories, 148
Symptoms, 148, 151, 191, 209, 211-215, 219, 232, 234

T
Tantrums, 163-165, 172
Teething, 139, 154, 157, 203, 208
Telephone, 5-6, 14, 16, 77, 79, 87, 95-96, 202, 218, 226-227

Temperature, 44, 88, 94, 196-197, 205, 208-210, 213, 216, 219-222
    Auxiliary, 210, 219-222
    Digital, 219-220
    Oral, 213, 220, 222
    Rectal, 219-221, 228
Tepid, 40-41, 196-197, 205-206, 210, 221-222
Termination Friction, 11
Terrible twos, 108, 137, 165
Territorial, 14
Theoretical, 29
Therapeutic Attitude, 60
Thermometer, 219-222, 228
Thrush, 154, 209
Thumb sucking, 155
Toddler, 15, 30, 94, 140, 163, 165-166, 168, 171-172
Toxic, 87
Toys, 23, 35-36, 41, 44-45, 47-48, 50, 53, 67, 71, 84, 86, 91, 94-95, 103, 127, 131-133, 139-141, 166, 170, 218, 246
    Age appropriate, 52
    Choosing, 139, 141, 180, 203
    Durability, 140
    Educational, 19, 84-85, 100, 133
    Hygiene, 22-23, 27, 31-32, 35, 48-49, 70, 147, 153, 195, 202-205, 207, 211, 242-243, 245
    Play value, 141
Training, 19, 29, 67, 70, 128, 159-162, 219, 234, 251
Transition, 4-5, 7, 14, 18, 29, 108, 115
Trash, 48, 247
Traumatic, 18, 136
Traveling, 17
Tremors, 156
Trust, 77, 107-108, 114, 236
Tylenol, 209, 213, 222

U
Umbilicus, 152-153, 195, 197, 199
 Umbilicus cord, 152
United States Pharmacopoeias*****

V
Vacation, 12, 17, 231, 234
Values, 74-76, 78, 113, 132, 235
Vegetarian, 183
Verbal environment, 122-123
Verbal, 17, 58, 122-123, 163, 192
Viral, 216
Visit, 17-18, 48, 95, 100, 104-105, 203-204
Vitamins, 180-181, 193-194
Vomiting, 155, 216, 228

W
Wash, 15, 32-33, 36, 38, 40-42, 48-50, 130, 148, 152, 154, 156, 195, 197, 199, 202-203, 205, 210, 212-213, 221-222, 243-246, 249-250
Water, 35, 39-42, 50, 87-88, 94, 97, 103, 130, 150, 152, 154, 181-182, 191, 195-197, 205, 210, 216, 221-222, 243-246, 249-250
 Main, 15, 43, 46, 97, 161, 180, 191
 Safety, 6, 8, 21, 86, 90, 92-93, 97-98, 100, 103-105, 139-140
Weight gain, 187
Window guard, 95
Work agreement, 4, 11
Work responsibilities, 9
Worksheet, 32-33, 35
www.professionalnanny.com, 4, 19

0-595-26138-8